The Complete Guide to Wills

What You Need to Know Explained Simply

Linda C. Ashar, attorney at law and Sandy Baker

THE COMPLETE GUIDE TO WILLS: WHAT YOU NEED TO KNOW EXPLAINED SIMPLY

Library of Congress Cataloging-in-Publication Data

Ashar, Linda C., 1947-
  The complete guide to wills : what you need to know explained simply / by Linda C. Ashar and Sandy Baker.
    p. cm.
Includes bibliographical references and index.
ISBN-13: 978-1-60138-312-9 (alk. paper)
ISBN-10: 1-60138-312-6 (alk. paper)
1. Wills--United States. I. Baker, Sandy Ann, 1976- II. Title.
KF755.A97 2011
346.7305'4--dc22
                            2011011350

Printed in the United States

PROJECT MANAGER: Melissa Peterson • ASSISTANT EDITOR: Angela Pham
INTERIOR LAYOUT: Antoinette D'Amore • addesign@videotron.ca
PROOFREADER: Gretchen Pressley • gpressley@atlantic-pub.com
COVER DESIGN: Meg Buchner • meg@megbuchner.com
BACK COVER DESIGN: Jackie Miller • millerjackiej@gmail.com

Printed on Recycled Paper

A few years back we lost our beloved pet dog Bear, who was not only our best and dearest friend but also the "Vice President of Sunshine" here at Atlantic Publishing. He did not receive a salary but worked tirelessly 24 hours a day to please his parents.

Bear was a rescue dog who turned around and showered myself, my wife, Sherri, his grandparents Jean, Bob, and Nancy, and every person and animal he met (well, maybe not rabbits) with friendship and love. He made a lot of people smile every day.

We wanted you to know a portion of the profits of this book will be donated in Bear's memory to local animal shelters, parks, conservation organizations, and other individuals and nonprofit organizations in need of assistance.

– Douglas & Sherri Brown

PS: We have since adopted two more rescue dogs: first Scout, and the following year, Ginger. They were both mixed golden retrievers who needed a home.

Want to help animals and the world? Here are a dozen easy suggestions you and your family can implement today:

- *Adopt and rescue a pet from a local shelter.*
- *Support local and no-kill animal shelters.*
- *Plant a tree to honor someone you love.*
- *Be a developer — put up some birdhouses.*
- *Buy live, potted Christmas trees and replant them.*
- *Make sure you spend time with your animals each day.*
- *Save natural resources by recycling and buying recycled products.*
- *Drink tap water, or filter your own water at home.*
- *Whenever possible, limit your use of or do not use pesticides.*
- *If you eat seafood, make sustainable choices.*
- *Support your local farmers market.*
- *Get outside. Visit a park, volunteer, walk your dog, or ride your bike.*

Five years ago, Atlantic Publishing signed the Green Press Initiative. These guidelines promote environmentally friendly practices, such as using recycled stock and vegetable-based inks, avoiding waste, choosing energy-efficient resources, and promoting a no-pulping policy. We now use 100-percent recycled stock on all our books. The results: in one year, switching to post-consumer recycled stock saved 24 mature trees, 5,000 gallons of water, the equivalent of the total energy used for one home in a year, and the equivalent of the greenhouse gases from one car driven for a year.

Table of Contents

Chapter 7: The Executor 123

Chapter 8: Providing for Children by Will...... 139

Chapter 12: Medical Decisions and Incapacity...... 199

Chapter 13: Final Life Decisions 215

Conclusion...221

Appendix A: Estate Planning Worksheets 223

Introduction

T he last will and testament — a person's final directive for the disposal of property and personal effects according to his or her "will" — is a more profound documentary of a person's life than people realize or consider. Whether standing by itself or as a component of a more comprehensive estate plan, the will gives a person the opportunity to maintain final control over his or her affairs, define a plan for the future of others in the person's life, reward those who have meaning in his or her life, care for those who depend upon him or her, and explain his or her final wishes.

A person's will, when properly prepared and executed, is a legal document of serious weight and importance. Courts must enforce it. The deceased — the testator — is no longer alive but still speaks through the will and the court, and others must listen.

Many people shy away from preparing a will for a variety of reasons, including:

"It is too difficult."

"I do not own enough property to make it worth the effort."

"Wills are for the rich."

"I do not know where to start."

"I'm too young to need to worry about a will."

Perhaps some may intend to prepare a will and just never get around to it. President Abraham Lincoln, a consummate lawyer, died without a will. Although he did not know he would be assassinated the day it happened, Lincoln certainly knew his life was in danger. Yet this did not motivate him to make a will.

Lincoln's personal motives are unknown, but the most compelling — and likely truthful — reason most people avoid making their wills is the visceral tendency to shy away from the whole notion of their own mortality. People know death is inevitable, but planning for it can seem ghoulish or morbid at the worst, and at the least, distasteful. Some are superstitious and believe to write a will tempts fate to hasten their death. Regardless of such reasons, spending time drafting out the "what ifs" in case of one's own death is not high on the weekend to-do list.

None of these are good reasons to refuse making a will. Anyone can make a will. Everyone should. A will can prevent a lot of confusion and save trouble for people left behind. It brings certainty to the chaotic emotions and disarray of affairs that follow in the wake of a death. It gives the testator final control of his or her property if there are no heirs to leave behind. The will can preserve items important to the testator; it can communicate his or her important ideas.

Wills have been recognized as important legal documents since ancient times. They existed in ancient Greece and Rome. Evidence of an oral will pronounced from a deathbed is found as early as in the Bible, in *Genesis 48*, in which Jacob bequeaths his lands and the future of Israel to Joseph, his sons, and his brethren. Inheritance rights of descent and distribution are an enduring concern of law and society.

One of the oldest written wills was unearthed in Egypt by the English archeologist William Petrie. Dated at approximately 2550 B.C., this will was written by an Egyptian named Sekhenren, who left his estate to his brother, a priest of Osiris. In some respects, our modern law of wills is directly traceable to ancient Roman law, which came along more than 2,000 years later, and even more recently to the English common law.

In the United States today, the laws governing the making and administering of wills are contained in the statutes of each state. Although there are common general principles across state lines, each state's law has its own unique features. For example, some states still recognize deathbed oral wills — called nuncupative wills — under certain circumstances and if they afterward are conformed to a written will as prescribed by law. Many states, though, have abolished oral wills.

Wills, then, must be in writing and prepared with forethought. They can be stand-alone testamentary documents or part of an estate plan that also includes trusts, insurance, and death benefit instruments that are self-executing apart from the will. Whether a person needs a simple will or something more complex should be a question answered with assistance of legal counsel, ideally counsel who specializes in the field of probate and estate planning.

Will preparation should begin with the testator making an inventory that answers two seemingly simple questions: "What do I have?" and "Where do I want it to go?" These questions encompass more than determining the next home for the family's prize heirlooms, though. There might be other considerations important to the testator, such as guardianship of minor children, care of adult dependents, provision for pets, or arrangement for charitable donations. Additionally, there are the legal formalities of drafting a will so it will be accepted and enforced by the court. It is important to understand how these goals and desires are set down in a legally enforceable document to ensure they will be carried out according to the testator's intent.

The testator's goals can be far reaching. People have used wills to further their social and scientific interests. The Nobel Prize was established in the will of Alfred Nobel, for example. Others have scorned family in favor of beloved pets. One of the most famous will controversies in this regard was the estate of hotel queen Leona Helmsley, who bequeathed $12 million to a trust for her Maltese dog, Trouble. She left nothing to her grandchildren, which triggered a will contest against her estate, worth billions. The court eventually cut Trouble's share to $2 million and awarded $6 million to the grandchildren. The remaining $4 million from Trouble's share went into a charitable trust. Thus, although a person generally has a free hand in declaring his or her intent in the will, there can be limitations. The Leona Helmsley estate illustrates the limits on bequests for the care of specific animals. Most states now have "pet trust" statutes to assist those who wish to cover this issue while planning their estate.

People often have used their wills, as well as trusts, to attempt to maintain control from the grave matters that are important to them. Often referred to as "incentive" provisions, such clauses in wills are designed to impose on others a certain lifestyle of thrift, health, morality, or achievement of specific goals. Examples are conditioning receipt of a sum of money upon enrolling in college, getting married within a year, refraining from smoking, becoming a teetotaler, or visiting the testator's grave on a certain date every year. Such provisions can be challenged for reasonableness, but they are presumed to be enforceable unless proved otherwise. The testator's intent is a powerful consideration. State laws also limit disinheriting spouses and impose a trust arrangement on the inheritances received by minor children, as well as appointment of their guardianship.

An estate need not be worth billions to require expert consideration for preparing a will. If one is not a mechanic, one obtains the services of someone who is a mechanic to make sure the car will run well and not break down before the trip has ended. The same common sense applies to organizing one's last will and testament. Individual state laws, tax law, misconceived myths and notions about writing a will, and the probate process all require a person to be informed about the choices and ramifications that can affect the drafting of the last will and testament. Each person's situation will have its own specific facts; each person's last "will" for his or her affairs will be unique. To understand what can and cannot be done and at what cost, the testator should select a knowledgeable advisor to assist with estate planning. An estate plan designs the management of assets and liabilities of a person with the goal of conserving and distributing his or her wealth after death. An estate plan might need only a will.

In addition to the will, though, an estate plan might include a trust, a legally binding written agreement that holds assets and manages them for a particular beneficiary or group of beneficiaries. The trust is administered by a person called a trustee or a number of persons who act as co-trustees. It is the trustee's job to manage the assets in the trust and make sure they are distributed in accordance with the instructions that govern the trust. Each trust has its own set of directions, determined by the person who created it, also called the settler, grantor, or trustor.

This book outlines the major considerations and features of wills and related estate planning elements. It is not legal advice. It does provide a baseline of information to help the reader formulate a plan and obtain legal advice to finalize that plan from a position of knowledge and self-understanding.

Chapter 1

Your Will and its Importance

A will is a legal document that dictates the disposition of your estate after death. A will can be a simple one-page declaration that all property and assets shall go to one named person — a spouse or a child for example. It can also be a complex document that lists many bequests, conditions, and provisions relating to your last wishes for your estate.

To be legally binding, a will must contain specific declarations that evidence it is intended to be regarded as the writer's last will and testament as opposed to simply a list of ideas not yet finalized. In legalese, the will's author is called a *testator*.

Be in Control

A will directs what will happen to the testator's property or assets. Many people misunderstand the term "assets" to mean only those items having formal title or residing in a financial institution. Thus, those who do not perceive themselves as wealthy assume they have no assets worth committing to a will. In reality, though, most people do have at least some items that will be subject to distribution to others upon their death. Only the testator fully knows and understands what he or she owns and its value. It is worth resolving what happens to these items by a will. Thus, in traditional legal terms, it is said that the testator must know "the measure of his bounty."

Simply stated, any property individually or jointly owned by the individual is an asset. Assets include (but are not limited to) homes, vehicles, vested interests in pensions or retirement plans, insurance policies, real estate, investments, stocks, bonds, cash, promissory notes (as the lender), and personal property such as furniture, clothing, jewelry, rugs, collectibles, and paintings. Some of the things about which surviving relatives and other interested persons argue the most passionately are items of special meaning beyond their monetary value: Mom's wedding dress, Dad's diaries, Grandma's antique settee, the buckeye tree in the front yard, Grandpa's watch. These things cannot be cut up and distributed in parts and still retain their intrinsic value.

Additionally, parents should consider the appointment of guardians of their minor children. Who is the best person to make decisions about the children's care and lifestyle? With whom are the children comfortable? Often, people request appointment of separate guardians for financial care and custodial care of their children. As well, those with elderly parents or disabled adult relatives might need to provide for their financial well-being. Some people might readily understand these considerations, while others might require advice to fully explore all available options and opportunities.

Without a will, a person dies "intestate." In this situation, state law directs who inherits the decedent's property and in what order of priority. This form of inheritance is called intestate succession. Some assume that if there is a surviving spouse, all will go to the spouse and there need not be a will to say so. However, although the surviving spouse indeed stands first in line under intestate succession, he or she will not necessarily inherit "all" by statute in every state. If there are also surviving children, for example, the intestate succession laws typically divide the estate among the spouse and children. Some people believe a life partner will be treated as a spouse, even though there was no official marriage. This is unlikely in most states. Another issue is whether there are unknown children who might show up after the parent dies. These are just a few of the many unanticipated, but possible, wrinkles that can arise when a person dies intestate. All of them can be addressed with certainty, according to the testator's choice, in a will.

Another intestate problem arises when survivors who inherit as a group do not agree among themselves about tangible assets that cannot be physically divided. These assets will have to be sold so the cash value obtained can be divided equally among them. Did Dad intend for his antique boat to be sold or did he just assume his only son would get it because they worked on it together while his two daughters showed no interest in it? Assume Dad is a widower, and his three children are then his intestate survivors. If Dad does not make a will, his son is not his sole survivor by statute. If the three siblings cannot come to an agreement about the boat, it will have to be sold, that is, liquidated for cash. The boat will not go to the son as Dad might have wished, and additionally it might not bring what Dad would have thought it was worth in the ultimate sale, but Dad did not make a will to foreclose this outcome.

Also, intestate probate procedure is often more costly than testate (will) proceedings because it generally requires more paperwork and forms than when probating a will. Further, taxes can be minimized by advance estate planning. Such legal tax-avoidance measures will not be an option for an intestate estate.

It can readily be seen that a will can provide a means for a person to communicate clear information and directions about his or her possessions, debts, other obligations, and final wishes. A will prevents leaving the resolution of an estate to unknown future circumstances without forethought. Whether simple or complex, a will is an important document. It need not be a puzzle or an undue burden to prepare.

In planning an estate, a person might conclude additional mechanisms such as a trust are beneficial for tax purposes or for providing for dependents. In addition to a will and trust, many estate plans also include a durable power of attorney, which defines who will make decisions regarding the affairs of a person who becomes mentally incompetent during his or her lifetime. Additionally, a durable health care power of attorney, living will, health care proxy, or advance health care directive can be implemented to make end-of-life decisions, such as use or withdrawal of life support, organ donation, and other medical choices. The powers of these documents end at death.

Although the various options for estate plans are worth knowing, it is first important to understand the foundation of the estate plan — the will.

Wills are not limited to the elderly, ill, rich, or famous. Death does not discriminate by age or social standing. Anyone who has reached the statutory age for making a will has the right to do so. In the majority of states, this is age 18. A few states will recognize a younger person's capacity to make a will, either by a specific age declared in the state's probate code (age 14 in Georgia, for example) or by recognition of a minor's emancipation to adult status under certain circumstances, such as marriage, evident independent self-sufficiency, parenthood, or military service. *Appendix D lists the minimum age for making a will in each state.*

Plan for children

Parents of minor children especially should consider the importance of making a will to clearly declare their wishes of guardianship and financial provisions for the children. Through their wills, parents can place the well-being of their children in trust to person(s) of their choosing after careful consideration.

Who will care for the children if something happens to both parents? Should their guardian be a sister, a grandparent, or someone else? Should different people be involved in financial oversight versus personal care of the children? Not all states automatically recognize a guardian named in a will because the final determination is made by the court. Even so, the parents' wishes stated formally in the will carry great weight in the court's consideration. It can be an additional comfort for the children that their parents are able to still speak for them.

The will also can delineate other aspects of caring for the children: it can encompass a trust to financially provide for the children until they are out of college or perhaps help pay for college. It can designate a sum of money for the children to receive when they each reach a designated age, and it can outline the specific goals the parents want for their children, such as tuition to be paid for a specific secondary school or college.

Without a will to express the parents' decisions and last wishes, if both parents die, there is a risk the children's placement will be left to chance. For example, if both parents perish in a car accident, the children could immediately be placed in the custody of a relative who is not someone the parents would have chosen. Or, there might be no relatives, which raises the need of state foster care. Later, the court will decide who gets permanent custody of the children. Through their wills, parents can speak for their children's welfare and futures. In some states, such as New York, parents can execute guardianship appointment documents in advance that will be honored in such a situation.

Plan finances

Another benefit of a will is that financial assistance can be provided to those left behind. It can provide for a spouse, children, and other dependents, and it can bequeath money or other assets to the testator's other relatives, friends, favorite charity, local business, group, organization, or hospital.

To effectively convey these benefits, the will must outline the specifics of such a plan. Consider, for example, a bequest for college tuition. Where is this money? Does tangible property need to be liquidated for it? What will this money do in the meantime? What happens to the tuition fund if the child decides to skip college? In situations like this, it is helpful to work closely with your estate planning attorney to ensure your financial wishes are met and contingencies are built into the plan to cover the "what ifs."

Plan for business interests

You have spent years forming your business, and you are passionate about it. Whether you own the next biggest department store or a start-up home-based enterprise, your business is something to seriously consider when it comes to writing your will and planning your estate. Every business owner should make key decisions early on so the business can continue, grow, and flourish when he or she is no longer in charge. Succession planning for a business can be done through corporate documentation. It can also be done by will.

What type of business do you have?

If your business is a sole proprietorship, it is a personal, individually owned asset, and the debts are also personal. If you own the business as part of a partnership or shares with others, the business is not solely yours, though you have an interest in your partnership share. Your ownership interest is your asset, but it can be fettered with limitations that are part of the business structure. The partnership agreement might require sale back to the other partners (redemption) for a predetermined value or at a value to be determined according to a predetermined formula. A similar redemption agreement governing ownership of shares owned in a corporation or limited liability company can be triggered by the death of a shareholder. In this type of circumstance, the estate value is not tied to the business operation but rather to the cash valuation of your ownership interest in the business.

Business ownership with others should be structured for such contingencies as death, as well as disability and retirement. This is called succession planning for the business. If no limitations on transfer of ownership are involved in the business structure, your interest will pass either by your will or, in the absence of a will, under intestate succession to your statutory heirs. This might not be in the best interest of the business or desired by the other partners or owners.

What stage is your business in right now? Do you have the best form of business ownership in place? If not, take the time now to organize the legal structure of your business. By doing so, you can make key decisions regarding your business in terms of your estate plan as well as defining assets and liabilities associated with the business.

If you are not sure your business is in the right form at this point, there is never a better time to make the necessary changes. It is also important to keep in mind that your business might need to change over time for one reason or another. Any time there are changes to the ownership of something you own, especially something as valuable as your business, it is essential you make corresponding updates to your will.

Stay Updated

Once your initial will is in place, you should update it in keeping with significant life changes, such as a marriage, the birth of a child, a divorce, the purchase or sale of property, or a change of mind about whom should receive certain assets. Amending your will is not difficult to do. Ideally, a will should be evaluated and updated, if needed, annually. You can amend your will by adding an amendment, called a codicil, to the existing will, or you can write a new will.

CASE STUDY: TIPS FROM AN ESTATE AND TRUST LITIGATOR

Phillip C. Lemmons
Fountain Valley, California
www.pcl-law.com
Author of Inheritance Theft: A Con
Artist's Guide to Your Inheritance

Phillip C. Lemmons is an estate and trust litigator practicing law in California. He has been working with wills and probate for the past ten years. He said, "wills and trusts are used as instructions for dissolving an estate after one passes away. They are important because they instruct executors and/or trustees to take certain actions regarding the payment of debts and the distribution of assets. If you don't have one or both of these instruments, the estate may not be dissolved pursuant to your desires."

Although many people have heard of the importance of writing a will, Lemmons also notes that trusts, part of the estate planning process, can also be just as important and less difficult to administer. "A will is administered during a judicially supervised probate process," he said. "Trusts are privately administered without any supervision."

According to Lemmons, the difference between an estate plan, a will, and a trust is that, "Wills and trusts are instruments used in an estate plan. A simple estate plan includes a will, trust, and powers of attorney." "Make sure it [the will] is done right, too," Lemmons stressed. "Otherwise, it may be invalid."

Accordingly, Lemmons noted the importance of power of attorney forms, as they provide individuals with an opportunity to determine who they want to make decisions for them should they become incapacitated. "Power of attorney forms are important because they provide another person with the authority to make financial or medical decisions on your behalf when you are mentally incapable of doing so. They are easy to create and execute. In most cases, they circumvent the need for a conservatorship." A conservatorship is a situation where a court appoints an individual known as a conservator to take care of legal matters for an estate or person.

Even before a will is created, Lemmons stressed the importance of a power of attorney form. The power of attorney gives another person the authority to act on your behalf. The person who authorizes another to act for him or her is known as the agent or attorney in fact. Lemmons noted that it is important to know that the power of attorney becomes invalid after the principal's death, "with one exception: if included, burial instructions will be honored."

Going through the estate planning process is extremely important. According to Lemmons, completing estate planning properly means using the right professionals to get the job done. However, if a person has no assets, he or she really does not need a will, Lemmons noted.

Chapter 2

Basic Considerations in Drafting a Will

here are various types of wills, as well as different ways in which property, needs, and wants can be addressed. All wills must be executed in a manner required by law to make them legal and enforceable.

Competency of the Testator

A fundamental requirement of a will is that the person drafting it must be *competent* to create a legal document. First, the person must be a legal adult — in most states, at least 18 years old. Some states still allow younger individuals to write wills, such as those who are married, in military service, or otherwise legally emancipated. Those under the age of majority should consult with an attorney about exceptions to the minimum age requirement.

Another essential requirement of legal competency is being of "sound mind." This is a phrase often heard in films portraying the reading of a will. It is indeed an important element. If an individual is not of sound mind, he or she lacks the mental capacity to make independent decisions that are legally enforceable. Therefore, a will drafted by someone who is not of sound mind at the time is not valid.

Whether a testator was of "sound mind" when writing a will is based on each state's interpretation of the concept according to the facts and possibly the terms of the will itself. First, the testator must understand what a will is and intend the document to be a will. Second, the testator must know the nature and extent of his or her property. For example leaving a million dollars to a favored nephew when the testator has no more than $1,000 to his or her name raises a question about competency. Disinheriting children with no history of animosity or estrangement and no explanation, and instead leaving all assets to an obscure (and questionable) charity, can also raise an issue of the testator's competency. Yet, it is rare for a court to invalidate a will due to incompetency without strong facts to support a finding of incompetency. The testator is presumed competent at the time he or she signs the will unless someone can prove incompetence. This is difficult to prove, especially because most people die long after they have put a will on paper. In the words of one court, "The law presumes sanity of the testator." Even a person who has been adjudged mentally incompetent and is under the care of a guardian or conservator can, in most states, make a valid will if he or she is in a period of lucidity at the time of making the will.

Another question that can be raised about competency is the allegation of coercion or undue influence on the testator to force a will or a trust to be drafted in a particular way. The family of an individual can fight the testator's decision in court on these grounds, but they will need more than mere allegations of impropriety to overturn a will. Individuals challenging a will must provide evidence that the requirements of a valid will were not satisfied and that the testator was subject to threats, misrepresentation, undue flattery, fraud, or physical or moral coercion sufficient to overcome the testator's free will. The person or persons' motive, opportunity, or even ability to control the testator will not be sufficient to establish coercion or undue influence unless there is also actual evidence that such control was in fact brought to bear on the testator.

Undue influence might be easier to prove, though, if the person accused of using it had a fiduciary or confidential relationship with the testator, such as, for example, a guardian, legal counsel, or trustee. A confidential or fiduciary relationship exists when the testator, afflicted by poor health, relies on the fiduciary to make critical life decisions and conduct business for the testator, especially in banking and other financial transactions. In such a situation, a presumption of undue influence could arise from evidence that shows the fiduciary relationship existed, the fiduciary benefited from the transaction (such as a substantial bequest in the will or transaction just before death), and the fiduciary actually had the opportunity to exert the influence over the testator's decision in the will's provision.

Will content

The document must also evidence intent that it is a will. This should not be a puzzle for a court to solve. The document should state that it is the writer's last will and testament; the date and place the testator made the will, the testator's signature, and witnesses' signatures should all be present. In some states, a holographic will, which is a will written entirely in the testator's own handwriting, is recognized. A holographic will does not require witnesses.

Next, the document must have at least one substantive clause that declares a beneficiary and the property bequeathed or other testamentary directive, such as nomination of a guardian for a minor child or creation of a testamentary trust. The shortest substantive clause of a valid will stated, "All to wife." This is not a recommended clause, but it illustrates the point.

A will should also name a personal representative, usually called an executor (if a man is named, executrix if a woman is named), the person responsible for carrying out the will's directions. The appointment of the executor is approved by the court when the will is offered for probate. If the will fails to name a personal representative, the court will appoint one.

When a will is written in any state, it is considered legally binding throughout the country, as long as it meets all requirements of the state in which it was signed at the time it was signed. For example, if the testator, a New York resident, followed the rules of New York and executed a valid will in Albany, but later moved to New Jersey, the will is valid in New Jersey because it is valid in New York. If there are changes made to the will after the move to New Jersey, the will needs to be updated or rewritten according to New Jersey's legal requirements if they differ from New York's.

Because a will could be voided on a technicality, legal counsel's advice on the applicable state's requirements for a valid will is important. Do not rely on Internet packages or store shelf bargain will forms.

To summarize, subject to variances in types of wills, and specific state law nuances, all wills require the following:

1. **A clear statement that the document is your last will and testament.** This makes it clear it is your *intent* that the document is to be considered your will.

2. **Statement of competency.** Although competency may be presumed in most cases, it is not something you should leave to chance. It is customary and recommended to recite that you are competent to make your will. A statement such as, "I am of lawful age, of sound mind, and know the measure of my bounty," is a traditional example that encompasses the elements of competency. Another term of knowing the measure of one's bounty is "being of disposing memory," which means essentially the same thing, that is, accurately knowing and recalling what you own so as to be able to "dispose" of it. Thus begins the last will and testament of Elvis Presley: "I, Elvis A. Presley, being of sound mind and disposing memory, do hereby make, publish and declare this instrument to be my last will and testament, hereby revoking any and all wills and codicils by me at any time heretofore made."

3. **Revocation of prior wills and codicils.** As noted above in Elvis Presley's will's introductory clause, clarity demands that each new will revoke all prior wills and codicils. This should be stated as a matter of course, even if you have not officially made a will previously. When you are gone, you will not be in a position to deny a proffered earlier will is a fraud. However, if your valid will revokes prior wills, you will have preempted such an eventuality.

4. **Date of the will.** There have been will challenges in some states over whether a will was properly dated. A date is important for many reasons. It establishes the testator was of lawful age. It places the will at a point in time should

other wills be offered to supersede it. It relates to what you owned at the time you made the will. It can relate to who was or was not a spouse, as well as whether later children were born after the fact. These are just some of the obvious reasons why dating a will is considered legally significant and required.

5. **Clause bequeathing your property.** The will must contain at least one substantive clause bequeathing your property.

6. **Signature of the testator at the end of the will.** You must sign your will or, if unable to sign, make a mark or direct your signature to be made in your presence with witnesses. In the latter case, state statutory requirements must be observed carefully.

7. **Witnesses.** Unless the will is a valid holographic will, your signature must be witnessed by at least two competent witnesses in your presence to whom you have declared the document is your last will and testament. Some states dictate that witnesses cannot be persons who inherit under the will or who are named as personal representatives in the will. Witnesses cannot be just anyone you grab off the street either, without first ensuring that they themselves are competent to act as witnesses to a will.

8. **An executor.** Your will must name an executor or executrix, or equivalent term for your state, to be the will's administrator.

The importance of witnesses

The law has a three-fold purpose for requiring witnesses to a will:

1. Witnesses, in addition to the testator, confirm that the document is a last will and testament (the paper is intended to be a will).

2. Requiring witnesses to appear and sign with the testator is a check and balance against fraud upon the testator, such as someone else forging a will in his or name.

3. Witnesses can give evidence as to the testatator's competency — for example, testamentary capacity — to make a will.

Many people believe that anyone can be pressed into service to sign as a witness as long as the person is not disqualified because he or she has a mental disability or is named in the will. The testator gathers the witnesses, says, "This is my will," and signs it and indicates the witnesses should sign under his or her name. Witnessing accomplished it seems. However, it is not quite that easy or such an indifferent a situation. *learn how to write!*

The danger of using whoever is at hand without being sure of the witness' understanding of the situation is illustrated in the 1917 Oklahoma case Hill v. Davis & Cobb. At issue in this case was the will of a testator who could speak and understand only the Creek language. There were three witnesses to her nonholographic will. Witness one and two could only speak and understand English. However, witness three could speak and understand both Creek and English. When the testator assembled with the witnesses to execute her will, she declared, in Creek, the document to be her last will and testament and requested they sign as witnesses to her signature on the will. Only witness three could understand what the testator said, so witness three translated and interpreted the testator's statement in English to the other two witnesses. Of course, the testator could not understand what witness three said in English to the other two witnesses, so she inferred that witness three was translating for her. All three then signed as witnesses on the will. However, after the testator died, the court denied the will for probate because only one witness to the will had understood the testator's words, and the statute required a minimum of two attesting witnesses. The two witnesses who did not share a language with the testator could not be competent attesting witnesses because there was no evidence they could understand each other. To the contrary, only witness three had a comprehensive firsthand understanding of the proceedings, and this was inherently legally insufficient to validate the will.

Types of Wills

With an understanding of what is required for a will to be valid, consider the following types of wills:

Standard witnessed will

The most common form of a will is created in typed form and witnessed according to the requirements of the state in which it is executed. Two witnesses are standard, but as noted, the requirements of who can serve as a competent witness must be observed.

Statutory will

A statutory will is created from a form expressly prescribed by state statute. *It is advisable to use this form only in that state.* Only a few states offer statutory wills: California, Maine, Massachusetts, Michigan, New Mexico, and Wisconsin.

The benefits of using these wills are that they are simple to fill out and usually inexpensive to put in place. There are difficulties with using this method, though. For example, most forms limit the options of dividing property. Because they are specific, there is little flexibility for the testator. The underlying problem with statutory wills is that the form is presented in a one-size-fits-all format, which might not fit your specific needs. For example, California's statutory will form does not provide the testator the choice of leaving the home and vehicle to different people. Other statutory wills have similar shortcomings.

So why use a statutory will form? If you have simple goals and wish to give most of your property to one person, you may find the form convenient, with the added assurance that the form conforms to a state statute for a lawful will.

Holographic will

As mentioned earlier, some states recognize an unwitnessed will that is written entirely in the testator's own handwriting. This is a holographic will. States which presently recognize holographic wills are: Alaska, Arizona, Arkansas, California, Colorado, Idaho, Kentucky, Louisiana, Maine, Maryland, Michigan, Mississippi, Montana, Nebraska, Nevada, New Jersey, New York, North Carolina, Oklahoma, Pennsylvania, South Dakota, Tennessee, Texas, Utah, Virginia, West Virginia, and Wyoming.

The primary advantages of a holographic will for most people are secrecy and convenience. Because it does not have to be witnessed, the testator can write it out and sequester the will without disclosing its existence to anyone. Such confidentiality is important to some people. Further, if circumstances are such that witnesses are not readily available, the holographic will offers an easy means of getting a will in place.

The idea of writing out one's own will at any time or place can be attractive, especially to those who are averse to discussing their business with others. This convenience factor, though, is fraught with potential problems. Writing a will without assistance can result in mistakes that might invalidate it. Crossing out portions of the will; adding other items into it after the signature; leaving out an essential element of a will; using language that can bring the testator's intent (or competency) into question — these are examples of issues that can arise with holographic wills when the will is presented for probate. Additionally, the will must be proven to be the testator's handwriting.

Validation that the testator indeed wrote the will and intended the document to be a last will and testament is the statutory purpose of requiring witnesses. To reduce the risk of forged wills, many states do not permit holographic wills.

Where holographic wills are permitted, there is no require-ment of a specific type of paper or ink, though quality materials are recommended for legibility and longevity. Something as serious as a will should not be relegated to such quixotic surfaces as watermelon rinds, pillowcases, and toilet paper. People have resorted to such ingenuity in strange situations, though. Writer Leo Tolstoy is said to have written his will on a tree stump. A Canadian farmer, trapped under a tractor in a field, wrote a brief will leaving all to his wife on the tractor's fender. He was rescued but died of his injuries a few days later. The court accepted the fender in probate as a valid will.

Those who have the option of writing a holographic will should do so with care and make sure the will is stored in a safe place where it can be readily accessed by the executor for probate at time of death.

Computerized or electronic will

In the age of the Internet, storing your will on the computer or CD-ROM seems like a good option. Yet, the only state that allows for electronic or computerized wills is Nevada. In this format, all of the information and the will itself are stored directly on a computer. There are some special requirements inherent with electronic wills. For example, the will must have a unique electronic signature to authenticate it. Examples of an electronic signature are a typed name at the end of a document, a digital image of a signature attached to a document, or a pin or numeric code that identifies a person. What is important to remember in the case of computerized wills is that the electronic signature must be unique to the testator. In addition to this, the state of Nevada also requires that the will provide an additional source of verification of the testator's identity, which could be via a retinal scan, fingerprint, face recognition, or voice recognition.

Video will

Video wills that stand alone are not legally binding, though Nevada's electronic will provision could feasibly include a video component. A video can accompany the legally compliant written will as the testator's explanatory message. A video prepared contemporaneously with the execution of the will could also provide evidence of the testator's competency.

Nuncupative (oral) will

Most states do not consider nuncupative, or oral, wills to be valid. Historically, such wills were recognized as deathbed declarations when a person did not have a will already in place or wished to make a change to a will. Today, those states that still allow them do so only under limited circumstances and require witnesses present to reduce the oral declaration to writing.

Typically, oral wills can only be used in situations where there is immediate danger of imminent death, and amending or writing a will is not possible. Another case in which an oral will can be binding, in some states, is if the testator is on active duty in the U.S. military. Further, oral wills are generally limited to convey only a small amount of assets. Reliance on this type of will to suffice at the last minute is obviously not the recommended approach to estate planning.

Oral wills are frequently challenged for either competency of the testator or undue influence. Competency questions arise, for example, from the circumstances of illness and presumed fear of death. Persons close to the testator might be accused of unduly swaying his or her thinking.

States that recognize some form of oral will at this time are: Alaska, District of Columbia, Georgia, Indiana, Kansas, Louisiana, Massachusetts, Mississippi, Missouri, New Hampshire, New York, North Carolina, Ohio, Oklahoma, Rhode Island, South Carolina, Tennessee, Texas, Vermont, Virginia, Washington, and West Virginia.

Although there are variances in details among these states, the general requirements of a nuncupative will include the following elements:

- Testator's expectation of imminent death
- Testator is competent and orally declares his or her will
- In the presence of at least two witnesses (might be three in some states and/or a notary)
- Will is reduced to writing by a witness and attested by the witnesses within time prescribed by statute
- Meets the monetary limitations prescribed by statute
- Filed with the probate court

Joint wills

When a married couple or life partners plan an estate, it is important that they consider what will happen with the assets (and tax consequences) when one dies and then the other, as well as if they die simultaneously or close in time. In most cases, the partners should have their own individual wills. This allows each person to specify his or her own wishes, even if each simply mirrors the other. Some states recognize the concept of a joint will, however. A joint will arises when two individuals share the same will in one document. This type of will, once executed, becomes a contract between the two persons. The document becomes more than a will because neither can make changes in the will without the consent of the other.

The purpose of a joint will is to lay out what both individuals have agreed will happen when one and then the other person dies. For example, if Joe and Mary are married to each other and create a legally binding joint will, the document will outline what will happen when the first of them dies and then what will happen after both are gone. If Mary dies first, Joe cannot change the will or make any changes to what happens with the property and bequests controlled by the will. Both have agreed to the will's ultimate outcome no matter who dies first.

Although such certainty and control are the goals of a joint will, they also can cause a problem. An example of a problem with a joint will is when one individual passes dies and the other subsequently remarries and/or has children. The original will remains in place with no provision for these new persons. The surviving testator cannot dispose of property controlled by the joint will or otherwise change the joint will.

Life can become complicated. It is not surprising, therefore, that joint wills have often been the subject of litigation. For this reason, lawyers tend to discourage their use and some states do not recognize them. Before entering into a joint will, consult legal counsel to be sure it fulfills a necessary purpose and that your state will enforce it.

Reciprocal wills

Unlike the joint will, reciprocal wills are an easier approach for spouses and life partners because these are separate wills that do not carry the binding contractual effect of the joint will. As explained by Indiana estate planning attorney, Paul A. Kraft, the reciprocal will is the "go-to estate planning document for most married couples. Based on the idea that a married couple will likely have the same wishes for their estate, their wills are created to 'mirror' each other so that no matter which spouse dies first, the estate is handled in essentially the same way."

The primary provisions in each reciprocal will leave the estate to the other spouse and names the spouse as the estate's personal representative. It is generally recommended that the will have a survivorship provision requiring the spouse to survive by 30 days to inherit and directing how the estate is to be divided if the spouse does not survive. This contingency prevents potential inheritance tax or probate complications. A backup personal representative should also be named in the reciprocal will.

Self-proved wills

You might hear the term "self-proved" will while planning your estate. This is a will that has a statement attached that has been executed by a notary public, or other person authorized to administer oaths in the state, attesting that the document is really the will of the person who signed it and that the witnesses to it properly witnessed and signed it according to law. In those states that recognize self-proved wills, this extra step eliminates the necessity of the probate court requiring witnesses to the will appearing in court to swear that they indeed signed the will in the presence of the testator.

In many states, a will is presumed "self-proving" as long as it bears the testator's and witnesses' proper signatures and is not challenged. If the will is challenged, though, the witnesses will be called to testify, if they are alive and can be found.

A self-proving statement is not part of the will itself; it is an attachment, separately signed, and sworn. Generally, where the self-proving procedure is recognized, a will can be self-proven at the time it is executed or at a later date. Michigan's Code Section 700.2504 illustrates such a self-proving will provision:

"(1) A will may be simultaneously executed, attested, and made self-proved by acknowledgment of the will by the testator and 2 witnesses' sworn statements, each made before an officer authorized to administer oaths under the laws of the state in which execution occurs and evidenced by the officer's certificate, under official seal, in substantially the following form:

I, _____, the testator, sign my name to this document on _____, _____. I have taken an oath, administered by the officer whose signature and seal appear on this document, swearing that the statements in this document are true. I declare to that officer that this document is my will; that I sign it willingly or willingly direct another to sign for me; that I execute it as my voluntary act for the purposes expressed in this will; and that I am 18 years of age or older, of sound mind, and under no constraint or undue influence.

_____
(Signature) Testator

We, _____ and _____,
the witnesses, sign our names to this document and have taken an oath, administered by the officer whose signature and seal appear on this document, to swear that all of the following statements are true: the individual signing this document as the testator executes the document as his or her will, signs it willingly or willingly directs another to sign for him or her, and executes it as his or her voluntary act for the purposes expressed in this will; each of us, in the testator's presence, signs this will as witness to the testator's signing; and, to the best of our knowledge, the testator is 18 years of age or older, of sound mind, and under no constraint or undue influence.

_____
(Signature) Witness

_____
(Signature) Witness

The State of _____

County of _____

Sworn to and signed in my presence by _____, the testator, and sworn to and signed in my presence by _____ and _____, witnesses, on _____, _____.
month/day year

_____
(SEAL) (Signed)

_____
(official capacity of officer)

(2) An attested will may be made self-proved at any time after its execution by the acknowledgment of the will by the testator and the sworn statements of the witnesses to the will, each made before an officer authorized to administer oaths under the laws of the state in which the acknowledgment occurs and evidenced by the officer's certificate, under the official seal, attached or annexed to the will in substantially the following form:

The State of _____

County of _____

We, _____, _____, and
_____, the testator and the witnesses, respectively, whose names are signed to the attached will, sign this document and have taken an oath, administered by the officer whose signature and seal appear on this document, to swear that all of the following statements are true: the individual signing this document as the will's testator executed the will as his or her will, signed it willingly or willingly directed another to sign for him or her, and executed it as his or her voluntary act for the purposes expressed in the will; each witness, in the testator's presence, signed the will as witness to the testator's signing; and, to the best of the witnesses' knowledge, the testator, at the time of the will's execution, was 18 years of age or older, of sound mind, and under no constraint or undue influence.

_____
(Signature) Testator

_____
Signature) Witness

_____
(Signature) Witness

Sworn to and signed in my presence by _____, the testator, and sworn to and signed in my presence by _____ and _____, witnesses, on _____, _____.month/day year

_____

(SEAL) (Signed)

_____

(official capacity of officer)

The same self-proving statements can be used with a codicil, which is an amendment to a will added without rewriting the entire will. Before using a self-proving device, consult an attorney in your state to be sure it is properly done according to your state's law. *A list of states that recognize self-proved wills, including those that have statutory forms, is included in Appendix D of this book.*

Making intent clear — explanatory letters

Ambiguities in a will raise questions about what the testator really intended. Courts then have to interpret a will to resolve the ambiguity. Ideally, the will should be drafted clearly to avoid ambiguities. There are additional things a testator might do that can be consulted if absolutely necessary to ensure intent is understood.

Some people use a video or an explanatory letter to explain why they made their wills in a certain way. This is not legally prohibited, but such supplemental information is not itself the equivalent of a will. Testators must be careful with such supplemental information so as not to raise more questions than are answered or bring their competency into question.

A common reason to do this is to explain why one person received more from the will than another did. For example, Grandpa leaves one grandchild, Bill, more money than another, Amy, in his will. His reason for doing this was to provide for Bill's continuing education, whereas Amy did not need this benefit because she had completed her education when Grandpa wrote his will. By outlining it in the explanatory letter, it is clear why he made this decision. Such explanation also could be included in the will itself unless there is a legal reason to exclude it. Generally, Amy would not have grounds to dispute Grandpa's not treating her equally to Bill, but his letter of explanation removes any inference that Grandpa loves Bill more than her or made a mistake in the will.

Explanatory letters are also used to express feelings of love, gratitude, or other personal sentiments that are not typically included in a will. Further, wills are public documents. Private letters are not. This reason alone prompts people to include explanatory letters with their wills to express feelings and convey messages they do not wish to make public.

If an explanatory letter exists, it can be mentioned in the will. As an example, the will of actor, Paul Newman, references an explanatory letter as follows:

"Memorandum: I may leave a memorandum containing suggestions for the disposition of certain items of my tangible personal property, but such memorand shall not be binding on the legatees named in this Section."

Ethical wills

Another type of letter a person might wish to leave behind is called an ethical will. This is not a legally binding will for disbursing; rather, the testator conveys thoughts, beliefs, values, and life experiences. This type of document is usually intended for children or heirs. It is not about property or assets but rather to pass down wisdom and philosophy. This document does not need to be drafted by an attorney, but it can be stored along with your formal, binding will and other personal papers.

Some individuals write far more in ethical wills than others and include stories, values, and beliefs they would like to share with family and friends. Ethical wills can also include photographs, videos, or other special mementos. Recording this information on video, CD-ROM, or audio file is an option for an ethical will. It is important that ethical wills and explanatory letters be internally consistent with the provisions of the last will and testament and estate plan. Ambiguities and questions should not be created. Just as the formal will is reviewed and revised from time to time, letters and ethical wills might need to be updated as well.

Living wills

A living will is a different type of "will." Often called an "advance directive for health care," this will does not dispose of assets and other personal effects after death. Instead, it is a document that conveys the writer's wishes, while living, about the administration of medical life sustaining measures, such as resuscitation measures, machine-assisted breathing, and stomach tube feeding. As such, it has a place in estate planning.

With a living will or advance directive, you can direct that specific measures be withheld, or provided, under certain circumstances. A similar but narrower type of document is the do not resuscitate (DNR) order, which forbids health care providers and family members responsible for your care from attempting to revive you from a stopped heart or breathing. Another decision that triggers an important action immediately at point of death is organ donation authorization.

These types of directives can be put in place in advance with appropriate documents according to the law of the state of residence. In addition, federal law requires that a person be advised of the right to make an advance directive for health care upon admission to a health care facility that takes Medicare or Medicaid. Thus, these facilities, regardless of state law, must recognize the concept of personal decisions to end treatment in terminal health situations.

Michigan, Nebraska, New York, and Massachusetts' state statutes do not expressly provide for living wills or advance directives for health care. This means health care providers in these states technically do not have to honor these directives unless federal law prevails. Instead, these states allow for such decisions to be made on a person's behalf by a health care proxy — in Massachusetts and New York — or health care advocate — in Michigan. A proxy or advocate is a person appointed under a durable health care power of attorney to act on behalf of another and make health care decisions when the patient is unable to do so, including decisions involving life-sustaining measures. Nebraska also provides for health care decisions for the terminally ill by a representative holding the patient's durable health care power of attorney.

Although health care providers in these four states are not absolutely mandated by law to honor living wills, the overwhelming national trend clearly favors them. The Michigan State Bar Association provides forms for an advance directive for health care and indicates it will be honored, despite Michigan's absence of an express statute on point.

In the states that recognize advance directives or living wills, these documents are expressly legally binding on the medical staff and family who are responsible for the person's care. Many states provide statutory forms for advance directives for health care, including Alabama, Arkansas, California, Connecticut, Delaware, Florida, Hawaii, Illinois, Indiana, Kentucky, Louisiana, Minnesota, Missouri, Montana, Nevada, New Hampshire, New Mexico, North Carolina, North Dakota, Oklahoma, Oregon, Pennsylvania, Rhode Island, South Carolina, South Dakota, Texas, and Washington.

As noted above, an alternative mechanism to the living will is the durable health care, by which a person designates someone to act on his or her behalf if he or she becomes incompetent to make decisions.

It is important to consult legal counsel for preparing a living will/advance directive for health care, durable health care power of attorney, or health care proxy, as nuances of legal requirements and forms differ from state to state. Further, the laws continue to evolve in this area.

Note: There is no reason to purchase forms on the Internet or in bookstores for a living will, advance directive, proxy, power of attorney, or any other related form. Free forms are available either online or by contacting the state's bar association or department of health and human services, or equivalent government office. Also, beware of generic "form services" because these do not conform to specific states and/or personal situations. Forms are useful to provide you a starting point because they can familiarize you with terms and general format. Every person's situation and personal beliefs are unique. Moreover, any person who has a complicated personal situation, such as close family members with opposing views, concerns about health care professionals not honoring agreements, lack of close family, or any other discomfort or doubt about this process should obtain legal counsel to assist and advise about all the choices involved and ensure the completed document will be enforceable. *Examples of a simple durable health care power of attorney and advance directive for health care are included in Appendix C of this book, for illustrative purposes.* Be sure to investigate what is required for your own state.

Pet Trusts

For those with pets, ensuring care for them after their owners' deaths is a common and responsible concern. An animal cannot be a named as a direct beneficiary in a will because it is not a human being. To the contrary, animals are considered property, the same as a chair or car.

To address this problem, many states have enacted statutes allowing for the creation of "pet trusts," which permit bestowing a sum of money for the benefit of a designated living animal. This can be done during your lifetime in anticipation of the future or within your will as a testamentary trust. A trustee is named to care for the pet and administer the funds on the pet's behalf. The trust ends when the pet dies. The limit on such trusts is that the sum bestowed must be reasonable to the pet's needs. Such was a consideration, no doubt, in the court's reduction of Leona Helmsley's $12 million bequest in trust to her dog, Trouble.

The following states presently recognize pet trusts by statute: Alabama, Alaska, Arizona, Arkansas, California, Colorado, Delaware, Florida, Georgia, Hawaii, Idaho, Illinois, Indiana, Iowa, Kansas, Maine, Michigan, Missouri, Montana, Nebraska, Nevada, New Hampshire, New Mexico, New Jersey, New York,

North Carolina, North Dakota, Ohio, Oregon, Pennsylvania, Rhode Island, South Carolina, South Dakota, Tennessee, Texas, Utah, Virginia, Washington, Wisconsin, and Wyoming.

In a state that does not expressly provide for a pet trust by statute, it is recommended that people consult with legal counsel about possible alternatives. Because animals are considered property, one solution is to bequeath the animal to a family member or friend with whom the testator has arranged in advance for care. This requires placing your faith in the person who becomes the animal's new owner, as your wishes cannot be easily enforced. In the pet trust situation, on the other hand, the trustee has a formal fiduciary obligation to carry out his or her responsibility to the animal. This area of law continues to advance. It is expected that all 50 states will one day recognize the pet trust.

The Probate Process

The process of carrying out what is in your will starts with the executor, the individual named in the will. A man is called an executor and a woman an executrix. For ease of reference, the term used here will be executor. The executor's first task is to locate the will if the testator has not left instructions or placed it with the executor. For the executor, its whereabouts should not be a secret. The testator should have told the executor and legal counsel where the will is located and provided them with at least a copy of it.

The executor's next duty is to determine whether the estate must go through formal probate, depending on the state law's requirements. In most cases, this will be necessary as a matter of law. However, if an estate is under a certain value and there are no issues concerning payment of debts or disputes among beneficiaries or heirs, a short-form expedited process could be an option.

Probate court can be time consuming if errors or confusing terms are found in the will or there is a will contest. If there is a will, the document will be presented in probate court, but as long as the will is valid, the process will move forward smoothly. If the will fails, (such as in the case of a forgery or a document held invalid as not executed properly, or there is no will at all, then the deceased will be intestate and the probate court will order the administration of the estate according to state law for intestate succession.

Thus, through the probate process, the courts determine whether the will is legally binding and then give the executor the power to manage the deceased's estate. The executor will use the proceeds of the estate to pay taxes and debts owed by the estate, take care of property, and distribute estate proceeds according to the will's provisions, but he or she cannot dispose of property outside of these requirements. In the event that the estate is not sufficient to cover the debts of the estate, the executor will not be liable for the remaining debt or to loss of bequests to beneficiaries.

The probate court also takes swift action, whenever it is possible to do so, to name the legal guardian of the deceased's dependents under the age of 18. If the will has put in place a trust for a child, the funds and/or property are distributed to the trustee, who will manage the trust for the child as designated by the terms of the trust.

The full length of the probate process can take as long as a year, perhaps much longer in complex or contested actions. After the process has been completed, the executor is able to distribute the property left in the will. The probate process is what it is in order to allow creditors to make claims, which must be paid, refuted, or settled. Once the estate has passed through probate, any claims against the estate are invalid. One of the requirements of the probate process is to give creditors of the estate notice of the decedent's death so they can file claims against the estate. This ensures that creditors have the opportunity to make their claims against the estate while it is in probate and allows the ultimate settling of the estate once adequate time and notice for claims have been provided.

As is further discussed in this book, there are mechanisms to avoid probate for certain types of property or through a trust.

CASE STUDY: TIPS FROM AN ATTORNEY

Donald Ray Burger, attorney at law
Houston, Texas
www.burger.com

Donald Ray Burger has been an attorney and worked with wills and probate for 19 years. Burger was admitted to the practice of law in Texas in 1979. In addition to being licensed in Texas, he is licensed to practice in the southern, eastern, and western Federal District Courts of Texas and the U.S. Fifth Circuit Court of Appeals.

Although Burger does believe it is important to have a will, he also points out that most people probably do not need a trust. "I recommend that everyone have a medical power of attorney, but only a few people need a general power of attorney," he said. "If you have a will, you can designate who will act as executor of your estate in probate."

To be more specific, Burger explained the different considerations that can go into choosing between an estate plan, a will, and a trust.

"A will provides a simple — and inexpensive — method of transferring ownership of your property. As the value of your property exceeds $1 million, tax planning becomes a consideration. Also, as the amount of your property increases, it sometimes makes sense to come up with more complicated designs to dispose of your assets. This creates a need for estate planning. Trusts are also used for estate planning and asset protection by individuals who operate businesses that can be sued."

In the case that a person has no assets, Burger said a will is still needed because most people have assets even if they do not acknowledge them. "There are very few people who truly have 'no assets.' A simple will is cheap insurance to make sure assets you have now or accumulate in the future will be disposed of as you wish and with minimal 'trauma' to your relatives."

That said, there are some very important things to remember when putting together a will or creating an estate plan. Burger believes this can play a big part in making the situation a good one or a bad one for those left behind.

"Most people want to leave everything to their spouses, and if their spouses die before them, to their children. Thought should be given as to how this bequest to the children should be handled, especially if the children are minors," he noted. "There are many restrictions under Texas law on the rights of minors to control and manage property. Because of this, a testator who has minor children should give serious thought to who will act as guardian or custodian for the minor. Also, under the Probate Code, a guardianship of a minor ends when the minor turns 18 years old. Many parents would not relish the thought of their 18-year-old child suddenly having control of a large sum of money. It is often better to create a testamentary trust that parcels out the money over a span of years to encourage children to attend college and become financially independent on their own."

The Home Inventory

A good place to start in will preparation is with a home inventory list such as one created for insurance purposes. Most insurance companies recommend a homeowner go through his or her property piece by piece and formulate a list of the contents of any value. This way, should there be a fire or theft, there is proof the items existed when an insurance claim is filed for the loss. This is also a great tool for preparing a will. A home inventory provides the contents of the house, by category, which makes it easier to account for the property to consider naming in the will. Useful with a home inventory is a set of representative photographs by album or CD-ROM, or a video, which individually lists each of the items. It can also be a list with detailed explanations of these items. For written lists, include any serial numbers on the items, if possible.

Thorough will preparation requires more than a household inventory. When preparing a will, the testator must be aware of everything, *i.e.*, real estate, financial investments, vehicles, bank accounts, intellectual property, collections, antiques, and so forth. It is especially important to make note of specific bequests for individual people.

In some situations, individuals have only a few items and wish to leave all they have to one person. In this case, it might not seem necessary to have such a thorough, itemized inventory of assets prepared for will planning. However, both the executor and the beneficiary will appreciate having a list of items to understand what they should expect to find in the estate. *For your convenience, a sample inventory worksheet is included in Appendix A of this book.*

Considering Special Properties

It is not uncommon for one person to own more than one property, which can make the will a bit more complex unless the property is deeded to pass outside probate. Examples of special properties include condominiums and timeshares. If you own these, there are special considerations to keep in mind when including these items in your list of ownership and in your will.

Condominiums are real estate, and as such, they are considered real property. However, unlike ownership of an unattached home, condo ownership can involve contracts with other individuals that limit the use of the condo. Although a condo can be sold like any other real estate, depending on the type of contract with the condo association, there can be restrictions concerning the property binding upon the next owners. Keep in mind that any condominium left to someone in a will still requires the new owner to abide by all requirements of the condo association. These requirements typically include association fees, improvement assessments, parking restrictions and other maintenance regulations. This should be a consideration when passing the property on to a beneficiary, especially if the plan is for that beneficiary to reside there.

Another type of special property is the cooperative living arrangement, or co-op. These facilities have a specialized concept of the residents owning stock in a company, which in turn owns and operates the facility. Monthly fees are assessed to keep the co-op running. In some states, co-ops are considered intangible property because the ownership is stock represented by a document, while other states consider it a form of real estate. Whether state law treats co-ops as intangibles or real estate will determine how this specific property is handled in probate. Real property requires more paperwork for transfer and ancillary proceedings if it is located in a different state than the testator's probate court.

Another type of specialized property is the timeshare. Timeshares are vacation properties in which someone "owns" only the right to spend a week or two per year in the particular property, usually a condo, apartment, or residence in a vacation resort. There are several types of situations concerning timeshares. One is a fee-simple ownership in which the timeshare holder actually owns a fraction of the property equivalent to the amount of time in a year represented in the timeshare. For example, if a person owns one week's timeshare, then he or she owns 1/52 of the real estate because the value is calculated on a year's basis. Your time period of ownership can be sold, rented, or gifted at your leisure. Fee-simple timeshares qualify as real estate.

The other common type of timeshare is called right to use. This type of property is considered leased for a certain amount of time, but it is not owned by the timeshare holder. This leasehold usually can be conveyed by will, but the timeshare entitlement will run out according to the terms of the lease. Timeshares can be bequeathed in your will to anyone, but they should be accurately labeled as to the type of property they are: fee-simple real estate or leasehold.

Condominiums, co-ops, and timeshares can be lovely gifts to receive in a will, but they can also be difficult for the new owner to sell due to restrictions on the properties and the inherent fluctuations of the real estate market. Real estate also can be costly to maintain beyond the beneficiary's means unless it is self-sustaining rental property occupied by a tenant. An option for probate properties is to direct the executor to liquidate them according to a plan and disburse the proceeds according to the will's direction.

Another option with real estate is to place ownership of such property interests in a joint survivorship arrangement with the intended beneficiary. Under this arrangement, at the death of either owner, the property passes to the survivor outside of probate and the property is not subject to the will at all.

Additionally, property can be placed in a trust. Property that generates income is especially suited for this consideration. The trustee is responsible for managing the property and disbursing income to the trust beneficiaries. When, or if, the property should be sold would be the subject of the trust terms, as decided by the trust grantor when setting up the trust. A trust can also be a useful device for property that is intended to be shared by children or other group of beneficiaries when there is concern of internal disagreement about use and maintenance of the property.

Where to keep the will

A will can be kept with the attorney who assisted in its preparation or, in most states, filed with the local probate court. Wills on deposit during the testator's lifetime are not public documents and can be retrieved and changed by the testator at any time. Putting the original will in a safety deposit box in a banking institution is not generally recommended. In some states, the box will be sealed upon death of its lessee (even where co-owned with another), which would delay the executor's ability to access the box to retrieve the will. A better practice is to keep a copy of the will in the safety deposit box as a backup should the original will be lost.

Your Estate Planning Team

Before you begin planning your estate and will, you might want to think about the people who can help you with this endeavor. Although this book is designed to allow you to do most of the work yourself, many people will want to seek additional support, including someone to handle their wills.

You might want to hire an estate planning team. This team can be as simple or as elaborate as you would like it to be. Depending on the size of your estate, your wishes, and your needs, this team might include the following individuals: an estate planning attorney, an accountant or tax professional, and an insurance agent.

Estate planning attorney

More than any other professional that you work with during this process, the estate planning attorney is the key person to have in your corner. He or she can help you with virtually every aspect of your will and legal matters.

The attorney you hire can:

- Craft wills in any form you need

- Aid you in designing trusts

- Offer legal counsel after you have completed your will to ensure it is legally binding

- Aid you in crafting attorney in fact and durable power of attorney documents

- Ensure your will is read, as they can hold a copy for you

- Provide you with answers to questions and aid you in complex scenarios

In many areas, you can work with a traditional family practice attorney. This individual will have decent knowledge of will design and basic trust design. If you have a large estate or a complex set of requirements, you might be better served to hire an attorney who specializes in estate planning. Although both the family practice attorney and the estate planning attorney will be good choices, those with more complex scenarios — and a bigger budget — might want to use an estate planning attorney for his or her expertise.

Tax planning strategies: Accountant or tax professional

You might want someone who can help you arrange your finances beyond the scope of just making payments. You can hire an accountant and tax professional whose goal is to minimize your taxes throughout your life and into your death. This professional can help you make decisions regarding how to invest your money to avoid taxes.

If your estate is large, you also want to consider someone who can manage your wealth when you are no longer able to do so. Although you might be expecting your durable power of attorney to list someone to manage your finances, remember that you might want an expert to manage your funds first, with your attorney in fact overseeing this individual's decisions and methods. This is no different than having an accountant manage your finances throughout your life.

By using these professionals, you can reduce your taxes and account for your finances today and well into your death. They can also help with creating documents for trusts during your life and after your death.

Insurance agents

As you work to build your wealth and care for your family, insurance products might be part of the package of wealth you are putting together. Life insurance policies, for example, can help you leave behind funds for your family to live off until they have accepted and dealt with the issues surrounding your death. In order to manage these insurance products, you should have a trusted professional by your side. It is imperative to select not just an insurance policy but also an insurance agent.

When you hire and work with an insurance agent, you can accomplish the following goals:

- Have your insurance agent help you decide the right policy for you based on your needs now and in the future

- Manage your insurance products for you and alert you of changes and updates you might need

- Talk with your estate planning team to help ensure all aspects of your insurance needs are covered and that all policies are up to date

- Work with your family after your death to ensure policies are paid in a timely manner and to the right people

- Help you to protect your family now for what might happen later financially

Insurance agencies are numerous, but finding an agent you trust and believe in takes a bit more research. You will want someone who can be by your side through the best and worst of it. You do not need an expensive policy just to pay the agent's bills. You need the right policy for you and your family.

What about financial planners?

A financial planner or estate planner is another person you might wish to work with as you prepare your will and manage your estate. These professionals do not necessarily design wills for you, but they do aid you in building assets to include. In most cases, you can work with them today so when you wish to retire in ten or more years, the funds are available to help you.

Financial planners are also a good investment if you have a large estate. They can help you make wise financial decisions; they aid you in making investment choices that will help you grow your estate, especially for your later years; and they can help you choose investments, plan your gifts for beneficiaries, establish your estate and any required trust funds, and manage retirement accounts.

When hiring these professionals, be sure they are people you trust because you will be staking a lot of your financial future on them.

Tips for Hiring Professionals

The four professionals listed in this chapter are people you might wish to include in your will and in the estate planning process. How do you hire the right ones? The following are some tips that can help you to do just that:

1. Research the professional and the company he or she works for intensely. You are putting a lot of your money and your wishes in his or her hands. You need to ensure this is the best person for the job.

2. Ensure that all professionals have up-to-date education, training, and licensing. Attorneys need to be licensed by their state to provide their services. Many states recognize the area of estate and probate as a specialty area of certification for lawyers and will list those with this certification with the state bar association. Accountants and tax professionals should be Certified Public Accountants. Insurance agents also need to be licensed by the state. Financial planners do not need licenses in some states unless they are offering specific investment advice. It is highly recommended that you work with a licensed planner for the best results.

3. Talk to the individual who will be managing your account. In most cases, you want just one person to be in charge of your assets. By doing this, you know exactly who to go to with questions or concerns. Interview this person to ensure he or she can make the decisions you require.

4. Learn of any affiliations these professionals have with third parties. For example, if you are working with a financial planner, he or she might push you toward investment plans that pay your planner a bonus for every sign up he or she receives. You do not have to work with these types of planners.

5. Ask for references and check them. If you do not know this person personally, you should learn as much as you can about him or her.

Hiring professionals to maintain your wills and estate plans is a good idea because it can give you peace of mind.

Chapter 3

Marriage and Wills — Important Considerations

arriage complicates the process of constructing a will because spousal rights to a portion of an estate take precedence as a matter of law. Some spouses have been known to prepare a will without regard to this limitation because they are seeking to disinherit the other spouse. Such a step puts the surviving spouse in the position of claiming his or her marital right by law "against the will."

In many marriages, though, the spouse will simply leave his or her belongings to the other spouse, which is a much simpler situation. However, for those who wish to leave some items to other members of their family or even friends, it is essential to know your state's laws regarding limitations on conveying property.

Keep in mind that in most situations, a spouse is not likely to complain about a gift given in a will. For example, a testator might wish to leave his or her treasured military medals to a son or a horse to a daughter. The spouse is not likely to contest such situations, especially if he or she knows about them prior to the reading of the will. Unless the surviving spouse has a marital claim or a joint property right to the property bequeathed to another person in the will, as long as the spousal share of the estate is satisfied, a spouse is not likely to prevail in contesting a specific bequest. Because of possible complications relating to marital rights, a testator is wise to make no assumptions and obtain legal advice about making such bequests.

Community Property States

States view the rights of married people differently. Some states define marital property as community property. Community property states presently are: Alaska (only if the couple has a written agreement specifying this), Arizona, California, Idaho, Louisiana, Nebraska, New Mexico, Texas, Washington, and Wisconsin. All other states and the District of Columbia follow what is known as common law as to marital property.

In the community property states, all property acquired by either spouse during the marriage is owned by both spouses equally. Each spouse owns 50 percent of the marital property. One important exception to this rule relates to property inherited by a spouse during the marriage. Inherited property, even if it is inherited during a marriage, remains the individual's own property and does not become community property unless it is commingled with the couple's community property so it can no longer be distinguished as separate property.

In community property states, property owned by one spouse prior to the marriage is also not part of the community property. For this reason, marriage partners should keep records of property they bring into a marriage if it is important to them that such property remain separate. In the absence of such records, proving its character in court, if necessary, can be difficult. This is one of the reasons why couples who have many assets prior to getting married enter into prenuptial agreements.

There are limited exceptions to the separate property classification. One typical exception is when spouses commingle their once-separate property together so it becomes difficult, if not impossible, to identify it from community property. For example, when Jordan marries Tom, she owns her own checking account with $20,000 on deposit in it. This is her own independent property at the time they marry. After the marriage, Jordan allows Tom to deposit funds into the account. Jordan also continues to deposit funds into the account. They both use the account to make purchases, and they both continue to put money into it. By adding funds to the account after marriage, the money in the account becomes commingled and contains both separate and community property. Because money is fungible, the property in the account has become too intertwined to easily separate the community property funds from the separate property funds. In this case, the account will likely come to be considered community property of the marriage. An inheritance of a sum of money, if commingled with marital property, can similarly lose its individuality. Marital partners who wish to retain the identity of their separate property should not mix it with community property and maintain a record of it.

What can a married person leave in a will in a community property law state? If you are a married person in one of these states, you can bequeath your 50 percent of the marital property and your separately owned property to anyone you please. For example, if you and your spouse bought a second home during your marriage, it is community property, and you each own 50 percent. You can leave your 50 percent interest in the home in your will to your nephew James. Upon your death, James will become a joint owner of the home with your spouse. They will be co-owners called tenants in common. Your spouse can also leave his or her half of the house by will to whomever he or she pleases. Or, both of you can agree to each leave your half interest to the other, with a contingency beneficiary of the property in case you both die at the same time.

What about income?

Income from separate, noncommunity property earned during the marriage can be a bit trickier to categorize because each state has individual rules about it. In some states, any income derived from separate property remains separate property. In other states, such as Idaho and Texas, income earned during the marriage from separate property is community property because it accrues during the marriage. The character of this income as either separate or community property will determine whether each spouse has the power to leave all or only half of it to someone other than the surviving spouse.

There are also specific rules regarding appreciated property value, businesses, monetary recovery from personal injury, and borrowed money. If you have any of these special circumstances in a community law state, it is best to consult your attorney about how these assets are affected by the law. Do not guess. However, the following are some items to keep in mind:

- **Appreciated property value:** Appreciated property value is a term used to describe the increase in a property's value over time. For example, your spouse might have purchased a plot of land ten years ago prior to your marriage. In the time since you got married, the property value has risen by 10 percent simply due to market appreciation. In most community law states, the increased value remains separate property. However, if there is a significant investment put into the property during the marriage that improves the property's value, the property can be considered community property. In this example, if one spouse purchased an empty plot of land prior to the marriage, but during the marriage, improvements were made by adding buildings to the lot, the effort is generally viewed as a marital investment, *i.e.*, community property.

- **Business property:** Business property can be classified as separate property if the spouse's only investment into the business was prior to the marriage, which is rarely the case. The problem in community property states is where the business increases in value during the marriage and the married couple has likely invested money into the business over the course of their marriage. The business property becomes community property because the funds are mixed. On the other hand, if the business is managed solely by one spouse, and no money is invested during the marriage, it arguably will remain separate property. The final determination of the classification of the business can be a long, complicated process of investigation better left to attorneys, accountants, and appraisers.

- **Monetary recovery from injury:** Suppose one spouse was injured in an accident and receives a sizable personal injury settlement. Is this property community property or separate property? It depends on the state. Most often, the amount of money received from the settlement will be regarded as separate property, but this is not always the case. The classification can depend on whether the other spouse caused the injury or has a derivative injury claim. In some states, the funds can have a different interpretation after death than during one's lifetime.

- **Borrowed funds:** Many people die owing some type of debt. Generally, in community property states, if a spouse has fully separate property and fully separate debts, his or her separate property will be applied pay off the separate debts. In addition, the deceased spouse's one-half of the community property can be used to satisfy debts. The problem here is it is often difficult to determine that a debt is separate property — which means only one individual is responsible for it. Whether a debt is separate property or community property depends on several factors. One of these is whether the debt existed before the marriage or whether the debt was indeed separately incurred by one spouse individually during the marriage. Creditors are likely to take the position that both spouses owe the debt.

Common Law States

In common law states, ownership of property in a marriage is determined by factors such as whose name is on the deed, who paid for the item, or who received the item as a gift. Unlike in community property states, in a common law state, property held by spouses is not automatically divided equally. You must look to actual indications of ownership to determine who owns the property in a common law state. Common law states give the surviving spouse the right to claim a percentage of the property left by the deceased spouse, if not provided for by will, but the surviving spouse's share is not always 50 percent.

This is because common law is actually formulated from the old English laws of the land in which women had few, if any, rights to the property of their husbands. Women could not write their own wills leaving anything they owned to someone else. Although this is not true today, the common law principles of property ownership are rooted in these old rules.

Are you planning to disinherit your spouse? You might want to rethink your plan because in common law states, there is protection for the spouse. In such situations, the disinherited spouse will have statutory rights to "take against the will." If you wish to leave your spouse none or a limited portion of the estate, the advice of counsel is critical to avoid a will contest that will likely disrupt your other bequests.

Waiver of spousal rights

There are times when a spouse wishes to give up his or her right to the spouse's property. Most common law states do allow this to happen. This waiving of rights is not common, and some states put strict restrictions on its use to ensure the spouse is not disinherited or disowned. Such a waiver of rights must be complete in writing, and it should have a signature with witnesses. One time this may be done is in a prenuptial agreement (prior to the marriage), but it can also occur after being married. If such a waiver is in place, the waiving spouse agrees to accept whatever his or her spouse leaves to them in the will.

"Taking against the will"

At the time of death, the surviving spouse makes a choice: accept what is in the will or pursue the process of "taking against the will" to obtain the surviving spouse's share provided by statute, a percentage of the estate's value. The process of taking against the will is a procedure done in probate court. A surviving spouse must be notified of spousal statutory rights to the estate as well as the will's provisions in order to make an informed decision.

Moving to Another State

Imagine you are living in a common law state and you move to a community property law state after your will has been put into place. Perhaps the opposite is true and you are moving into a common law state. There are various circumstances in play here including where you got married, when the will was written, what is in the will, and the differences between each state's laws on property.

If you move to the community property state of California, Idaho, Washington, or Wisconsin from a common law state, all property you own will fall under the rules of the community law state. Other states with community property laws do not recognize this process. Rather, the rules of the state in which the property was acquired will govern the ownership of property. In two community property states, Arizona and Texas, the law abides by the community law standards in this regard for a divorce but not necessarily for property gifted in a will.

Conversely, you could move from a community property state into a common law state. The rules here also differ somewhat for each state. One problem you might find in any scenario is that the court system is not standardized across all states. Therefore, if you have specific goals regarding the way in which you want property divided with your spouse, it is best to work with an attorney to put this plan in place before you die. In most situations, though, spouses are willing to leave at least 50 percent of their property to their surviving spouses. In these cases, many of these spousal rights rules will not be a concern.

CASE STUDY:
TIPS FROM A JUDGE

Judge Weldon Copeland
Probate Court One
Collin County Court at Law
University Drive Courts Facility
McKinney, TX

Note: These answers are generalizations and simplifications of complex legal issues. Every situation is unique, and you should consult your own lawyer before making any legal decisions.

There are many different sides to the probate story, and it is often helpful to look at the probate process from several different angles. Judge Weldon Copeland provided a look at the probate process from the opposite side of the courtroom long after the drafting of the will and the planning of the estate has ceased. Even though Judge Copeland handles the complexities of probate every day, he was quick to note that he has nothing to do with the process of planning it while presiding in probate court.

"Probate judges do little or nothing in the will planning and estate planning process," he began. "Occasionally, a probate judge will be asked to construe or modify the terms of a trust that was created in the estate planning process, but probate judges are not often otherwise called upon to take action in an estate planning matter. A substantial purpose of estate planning is undertaken to avoid — or at least minimize — probate court proceedings. Still, even good estate planning will sometimes leave a need for some minimal action in the probate court after a death."Judge Copeland did note that it is very important to have a will, trust, and designated power of attorney.

"The importance of having a will is determined by the circumstances and the intentions/desires of the individual involved," he said. "First and obviously, some people will want to pass their probate estates to one or more persons who would not inherit in the absence of a will under the descent and distribution/intestacy statutes. To pass an estate to another who would not inherit as an intestate heir, there needs to be a will or actions taken to place the deceased's assets into joint tenancies or trusts that will avoid the need to probate the estate. But even those who want to pass their estate to the people who would inherit under the descent and distribution/intestacy statutes will often desire to have the additional benefits that a will can provide."

Judge Copeland said that individuals can add provisions to a will that will streamline the administration of the estate and simplify many aspects of the probate process. For example, a person can name the individual who will administer the estate in the will and instruct that this person not be required to post bond. Without this designation in the will, a court may require that the executor post a bond to ensure he or she carries out his or her duties to administer the estate in good faith. The bond helps to ensure the executor does not commit fraud against the estate or embezzle any amounts from the estate. By designating the executor in the will and instructing that no bond needs to be posted, the testator removes a possible burden from the court and the shoulders of the executor. Similarly, individuals may also designate in their wills the person they wish to serve as the guardian of their children if both parents should die. This will eliminate the need for the court to appoint a guardian in such a situation.

"People with extremely large estates can achieve substantial tax advantages through trusts created in a will," Judge Copeland explained.

"Because the existence of a will can preclude access to the simplified small estate procedures under the Texas Probate Code, people with small estates will not require administration, and those estates worth less than $50,000, plus exempt property of any value, might be better off without a will. However, even those with small estates need a will if they wish to pass their probate estate differently than the intestacy laws."

Often the question is asked, "If a person has no assets, do they still need a will?" To this, Judge Copeland said, "There is no absolute 'yes' or 'no' answer. In Texas, probate proceedings are initiated for less than 40 percent of all deaths. The relative need for a will in a 'no-assets' estate would certainly be diminished in comparison to other estates with substantial assets, and it would be difficult to justify the expenditure of scarce funds for a will that may or may not be needed. Small estates present the greatest complexities in determining whether a person should have a will. As stated above, the existence of a will can preclude access to the simplified *small estate* procedures under the Texas Probate Code. People with small estates that will not require administration (less than $50,000 plus exempt property of any value) therefore will sometimes be better off without a will. Many estates are initiated for the sole purpose of appointing an administrator to bring a lawsuit against someone who has caused the death of our decedent. In these cases, the probate process could be simplified if there is a will. But these cases often do not afford an interval between the event causing death and the death itself, during which a will could be prepared."

Chapter 4

Life Insurance Plays a Significant Role

L ife insurance can be a means of funding an estate or taking care of a beneficiary. If the estate is the beneficiary, the proceeds will be subject to probate proceedings and costs. A better approach for this purpose is to have the proceeds fund a trust.

Why do you need life insurance? It might help you to have a larger estate. There are various types of policies, and it is true that some people will not need life insurance for long. Consider this: You are 40 years old, have two children, are married, and make the largest income in your family when you suddenly die in a car accident. Can your spouse make payments on the mortgage? Will your family be able to live the same lifestyle they have been living? More so, will your family suffer financial ruin because of a lack of funds from you? If so, a life insurance policy is necessary to lessen such a burden on your family.

As part of your estate and will, your life insurance policy can be one of the most important elements. In many families, most of the funds left by the deceased come from life insurance proceeds. Even if it is not a lot of money, this money is going to someone at the time of your death, assuming the policy is in good standing. Take some time now to consider whether you have life insurance, whether you have enough life insurance, and who your beneficiaries of the insurance are.

Life Insurance

You might be wondering why life insurance is even mentioned in a book about wills. Life insurance is a financial tool that can be useful in estate planning. How you plan to use life insurance benefits in the estate plan can affect how you structure your will and which beneficiaries you wish to place in your will. Life insurance can be used to cover debts that would otherwise deplete assets conveyed by the will. Another key item to keep in mind about life insurance is that income tax is not applied to the amount your beneficiary receives from your policy. Additionally, life insurance proceeds can be used to fund a testamentary trust setup in a will. In this arrangement, the trust is the beneficiary of the insurance proceeds. Another way of doing this is to create an inter vivos (life) trust that is the beneficiary of the proceeds of your life insurance. This trust can be minimally funded for purposes of creating it, or it can be an established trust you wish to further enrich with the life insurance benefit. Your legal counsel can advise you about the various ways life insurance can be used to fund estate plan options both within your will and outside of probate.

Is there benefit for you?

Purchasing life insurance is an intimate decision you must make for yourself. Asking the following questions can help you with this decision:

- **If you die tomorrow, unexpectedly, will your family have the means to live comfortably?** Even if you die 20 years from now, when you are 70 years old, will your spouse have the necessary funds to sustain life easily? If not, life insurance can help provide financial security for your spouse.

- **When you die, will your family have access to funds to pay for daily living expenses and provide for your funeral?** One thing often emphasized by insurance companies is the fact that pending tax matters and the estate proceedings may lock up funds at the time of your death, which would leave your family to fend for themselves financially because your funds are frozen. Even if your funds are not locked, though, there might not be sufficient funds readily available for all immediate needs. According to the National Funeral Directors Association, the average funeral costs $6,560 and $7,755 with the added cost of a vault. With the funds from an insurance policy, the family would have fast access to money they need to pay for their immediate expenses.

- **Do you want to cut out the IRS?** If you would like to leave behind money to your beneficiaries but do not want to have that money taxed as income, life insurance policies can be incredibly helpful because, as of the writing of this book, they are untaxed. In fact, you might even want to consider having a life insurance policy pay out to someone to whom you wish to give a gift, such as a grandchild.

- **Do you own a business relying on your success?** As a business owner, in some cases, your being there is what keeps the business running. If you die, will the business and each of its employees lose out financially? If so, you might wish to name your business or business partner as a beneficiary of your life insurance plan. By doing so, the business gets a much-needed cash infusion at your death until someone replaces you or someone else purchases it. This is often termed key-man insurance.

Types of Life Insurance Policies

You have decided that life insurance might be a good addition to your estate. Which type of policy should you have? There are a variety of possibilities. A good first step in searching for a policy is to check with your human resource manager at your current job about the possible life insurance policies your employer might already have purchased for you or have available for you to purchase. These are often an incentive for or benefit of working for certain companies. This type of life insurance is group term life insurance. If your employer does not offer life insurance or you feel like you need more coverage than your employer offers, you will next want to determine the best type of policy to fit your needs, and then you can determine the best amount of insurance to have.

Term life insurance

One of the most common types of life insurance policies is term life insurance. Term life insurance offers coverage for a fixed period of time. The fixed period of the policy can be from one year to several years. At the end of the period, there is typically the option to renew coverage for an additional period of time. The premiums on a term life insurance policy are typically lower than those for a lifetime policy. A term life insurance policy will only result in payment if you die during the term of the policy. Keep in mind that once the policy term is over, you will receive nothing from the policy.

The term life insurance policy offers a larger payout than some other forms. In addition, it is the least expensive type of insurance policy. The reason for this is that most people obtain term life when they are younger, and therefore, the risk to the life insurance company of the insured's death is far less than for an older individual. Any amount of insurance is available for purchase, ranging from as little as $10,000 up to hundreds of thousands, depending on what you would like to purchase. Generally, you will make an annual premium payment on the policy.

How much is term life insurance worth? Each person — as well as each insurance provider — determines this individually. The more insurance you purchase, meaning the larger the payout, the more expensive the term life insurance policy. As you get older, the cost of the insurance premiums will rise because the risk of your death statistically increases.

Within the larger canopy of term life insurance, there are several other considerations. Each of these is still term insurance, but there are different options to keep in mind.

- **Annually renewable term life:** As the name implies, this form of term life insurance is a policy that covers one year but is renewable at the end of each year at the election of the policyholder. Each year, you will see at least a slight increase in the premiums because you are getting older. The benefit of this type of insurance is that it often carries the lowest premium price.

- **Level term life:** Level term life insurance allows you to have the policy in place for a set number of years. Policies often include three-year and five-year plans, as well as those that last as long as ten or 20 years. There is a level of step-up associated with these plans. This means that when you reach a certain milestone, as defined by the policy, the premiums will increase. Another form of level term life insurance allows for the value of the policy to drop while keeping the life insurance premiums the same. Read these policies carefully to understand what is being offered to you.

- **Decreasing term life:** With decreasing term life insurance policies, the payoff value of the policy drops as you age. Meanwhile, the actual annual premium payment will remain the same. The benefit of obtaining a decreasing policy is that your annual living expenses are likely to decrease as you age. For example, when you are younger, your spouse needs a larger payout from the policy (should you die) to cover mortgage payments. As people age, their expenses typically are fewer, which means a lower payout of life insurance is acceptable. Thus, a decreasing premium makes sense for someone whose spouse will need less money to cover expenses after his or her death.

- **Mortgage term life or credit term life:** This is a relatively new type of life insurance policy. The benefit of this type of policy is to pay off your mortgage or your debt, as defined by the policy, at the time of your death. The term value of the policy decreases as the principal balance of your mortgage decreases. For example, if you have a mortgage term policy and you die during that term, the policy would pay off your mortgage and your family no longer needs to worry about it. This type of policy is usually more expensive than most other forms of term life insurance. The best reason to obtain this policy is if you have debts that would put your family at financial risk and you are unable to get insurance from another source. An example of someone who is uninsurable is someone who has been diagnosed with a serious illness. An insurance company is unlikely to insure someone with a high risk of dying early during the policy term.

- **Group term life:** As mentioned earlier, group term life insurance is obtainable as an employment benefit. Depending on the employer's benefit plan, you might contribute to the insurance premium through payroll, or your employer might cover the entire premium cost. You designate your beneficiary. Because of its affordability, you should obtain as much group term life insurance as possible. If you leave employment, you should have the opportunity to elect to continue the coverage as individual coverage at your own cost.

Term life insurance is a good option for many people but not for everyone. In fact, if you want to get more out of your life insurance, term life may not be the right way to go. Instead, consider a type of insurance that actually builds cash value.

Cash Value Building Life Insurance

Cash value life insurance is also known as whole life insurance. This type of policy offers a savings option. As mentioned earlier, you might want to choose a life insurance policy because it can help you save your money. In these forms of insurance policies, the value of the insurance builds up and splits into two sections. The first amount goes to the insurance company as the fee for the service and the second portion works as a savings account for you. There are several forms of cash value life insurance to consider.

- **Whole or ordinary life:** This is the simplest form of these policies. Here, you pay level premiums, and the value of the insurance policy stays the same over its lifetime. With each payment you make, a portion goes into the investment account while the other goes to the insurance company. The amount invested is predetermined, as is the investment form (where the funds are invested). As you accumulate money in the investment account, you are able to borrow from the funds, at a fee. Loans reduce the net cash value of the policy if not paid off at time of death.

- **Universal life insurance:** This form is similar to ordinary life, but the amount of the savings can fluctuate. The difference is in the form of investment made with these funds. The benefit here is you can change the coverage amounts as you need to in order to account for changes in your expectations about providing for your loved ones after your death. Be warned: this insurance is costly. Most of the premium goes toward the insurance protection rather than into your investment account.

- **Vanishing premium life insurance:** This policy hopes to help you to build your investment. At the beginning of the policy, the premiums are higher than normal. During these early years, you put more money away. The assumption is that as you put away large amounts upfront, that money will be able to earn a large enough return to cover part of your premiums in the future. The goal is that the early premiums will be large enough to earn interest to cover the entire amount of the later premiums. As a result, eventually you net paid-up insurance.

  Individuals considering this plan should be careful. These policies were widely popular in the 1980s and 1990s because of the attraction of vanishing future premium payments. However, your later premiums will only vanish if your earlier premiums are able to earn a return on interest great enough to cover the cost of the later premiums. It is highly likely, given current economic conditions, that the rate of return will be great enough to fully cover the cost of later premiums. In that case, you will be stuck paying the entire premium throughout the life of the policy.

- **First to die and last to die policies:** Instead of purchasing two separate life insurance policies for you and your spouse, you might be able to purchase just one. The first to die policy ensures that in the case of two people, when one of the insured persons dies, the surviving one gets a cash payout of the policy. Purchasing life insurance as one entity instead of two separate policies can save you money, especially because in many families, only the first to die policy is necessary.

The second to die policy is an ideal choice for those planning to leave the funds to an heir. It covers two people as well, but the benefits are not paid out until both of the policyholders die. The second to die policy is used for parents looking to provide support to their surviving heirs. The policy should cover estate taxes and works well as a way of transferring money to beneficiaries, rather than using the funds to pay for everyday expenses.

Now that you have an overview of the options in life insurance policies, how do you choose? Consider several options, but do not make a decision about any of them until you speak with a licensed insurance broker to discuss your options and which policies are best suited for the goals you have.

How Much Life Insurance is Enough?

When considering any investment in an insurance product, the question that stumps many is "how much?" The amount of insurance necessary depends on several factors, including what you want to protect with your insurance money and your overall goals for the policy. For those with term life insurance, you are likely covering your family for a set amount of time, such as when you have a mortgage. For those who purchase whole life insurance, the goal might be to find the most lucrative investment.

This is another decision you want to make with your financial planner and insurance agent. When hiring these professionals, be sure to research them carefully. It is exceptionally important to ensure you are working with a professional with no affiliation with any insurance companies or investors. You do not want them to promote a specific type or amount of life insurance to get a payout from these other companies.

Once you have a trusted agent to work with, you can get down to the process of determining which policy amount is best for you.

Replacing income

The majority of insurance policies purchased have a design to replace the lost income of the individual who has died. These policies are used to help pay for everyday costs, funeral costs, and other expenses the family might have at the time of your death.

The simplest way to know how much life insurance you need to replace your income for your family is to look at your finances. Consider how much insurance it will take to replace your income for your family over a period of time plus cover debt and death costs. Determining these costs will help suggest the amount of insurance you need.

Other potential goals

You might have other goals in obtaining a life insurance policy. You might wish to leave a sum of money to a loved one or you might wish to use a life insurance policy to protect your business. In these instances, it is essential to determine the amount of payout you would like to leave behind. For example, if you wish to pay for your grandchild's education, calculate the cost of a four-year college education, and do not forget to consider inflation.

If you are unsure of the amount of life insurance you need, work with a trusted financial planner to determine this. He or she is likely to give you various scenarios to consider that pertain to your individual needs and your overall financial goals. In addition, your other property and assets might also factor into this process.

Who is the Beneficiary?

Now that you have considered which life insurance policy is right for you and your family, you must make a decision on who will receive the funds from your insurance policy. This is not always an easy question to answer, but it should be an integral part of writing your will. One of the reasons life insurance plays a role in the process of writing a will is because it allows you to set aside money to specific people.

Ownership of the life insurance policy is also something you have to keep in mind. You want to pay close attention to the ownership and the beneficiaries because this will determine the control over the policy. If you purchased the life insurance policy for yourself, which is the most common method, you own the policy. Because of this ownership, you control the naming the beneficiary and are responsible for making the premium payments. Alternatively, another person can own a policy on your life, make the premium payments, and control the naming of beneficiaries. How you wish to organize your life insurance is a function of estate planning with advice of legal counsel.

When listing beneficiaries, there is no rule about who to list. You may wish to list your spouse, for example. Children and other relatives are also common. You can designate the funds to businesses and charities. It is also important to list alternative beneficiaries who have the ability to benefit from the life insurance payout if the primary beneficiary is no longer alive. For example, if your policy names your spouse as your beneficiary, but your spouse dies with you and you have named your child as the alternative beneficiary, he or she will be able to collect the payment. If you do not name an alternative, or you do not list enough alternatives, the proceeds from your life insurance policy become part of your estate under the residuary clause of your will and must go through probate court. At that point, the proceeds might be subject to estate taxes depending on the rules of your state.

If you wish to leave your life insurance to a minor child, the best option is to establish a trust for the child for these funds. The trust is managed by someone you appoint until the child is of the appropriate age to obtain these funds.

As with the rest of your estate plan components, be sure to review and re-evaluate your life insurance coverage from time to time. You can change your beneficiaries at any time during the policy's lifetime. You might wish to do this any time there is a major change in your assets or your family. As with any other part of your will and estate, be sure to keep records of your life insurance policies with your attorney or in another safe place. Avoid keeping these records in a safety deposit box.

Chapter 5

Pensions and Retirement Accounts

efore you start drafting your will, take a close look at your assets. Do you have or expect to have a pension or retirement plan? If so, this plan should be considered a part of your assets. Retirement accounts, pension plans, and other similar investments are designed to help you fund your retirement. Usually, these accounts are set up with a named beneficiary in case of death, who will convey the proceeds directly to beneficiaries you name to receive these funds outside of probate. If there is no beneficiary, however, your probate estate will be the default beneficiary. If you have not designated a specific beneficiary in your will, the proceeds will fall under the residuary clause of your will, which means the beneficiary is whom you have designated to receive the balance of your estate after specific bequests are satisfied.

Why does it matter what type of retirement vehicle you choose, and should you even think about this right now? The importance of having a retirement account is simple: You will likely need to have one for you to pay for your retirement. How you use that money and how you keep it defines who can receive any extra money left over from retirement. As part of writing your will, you should keep in mind all of these elements because they are a part of the big picture of your financial situation and who benefits from your death.

Qualified Pension Plans

While planning your estate, the term qualified pension plans might come up. A pension plan is almost any plan in which some of the benefits, which are provided by your employer, are set aside in a separate account to be used during retirement. A qualified pension plan is one in which the employer's investment into the plan is not taxed in the year it is placed into the plan.

More commonly, you will hear these plans labeled as tax-deferred plans. Tax-deferred accounts have no taxes levied on them at the time of the contribution, but when you pull the funds out in retirement, they are taxed at that time. Tax-deferred accounts are often beneficial because they are only taxed when the funds are taken out at the tax rate you qualify for at that time. Because you plan to retire and use these funds yourself, you might be in a lower tax bracket and, therefore, end up paying fewer taxes on the funds.

There are several types of qualified pension plans; each one is unique in terms of how you will consider it in planning your will and estate.

Defined benefit pension plans

Until recent years, defined benefit pension plans were the standard in terms of pensions. Now, many companies do not offer them. Pension plans like these are designed to pay out a specific amount of money every month after retirement. The plan might pay you $1,500 a month for the rest of your life, for example.

To determine how much you will receive in this form, review the plan documents and periodic statements or simply contact your company's human resource department and ask. Chances are they will provide you with a specific payment amount you are going to receive during your retirement. The years you have worked with the company, the salary you made, and other factors including the company's goals determine the amount of your payment.

Defined contribution pension plans

Defined contribution pension plans are similar to the pension plans previously mentioned except with defined contribution pension plans, the payments are not the same amount each month. Rather, the plan has a contribution of the same amount placed into it throughout your employment at the same rate. This is generally a percentage of your income, such as 1, 2, or more percent of your gross income. This has become the more common form of investment for most employers. The employer puts in the same percentage each paycheck — and you as an employee can contribute to that amount as well — and you choose how the funds are invested.

The employer will pick an investment company to manage these plans. Although the investment company is doing this, it is not making decisions for you regarding how investing of the funds occurs. This is because you, as the pension holder, own your own plan. You can determine just how aggressive or conservative you wish to be with your investments.

Profit sharing plans

If your company offers profit sharing benefits to you, it will pay you a set amount of money based on the company's profit take. These funds are managed similarly to defined contributions. Keep in mind that whenever there is a distribution to you from these funds, the funds are taxed at that time.

If you have questions about the type of retirement plan your employer has set up for you, talk to your human resource manager. Chances are good informational packets are available to you. If you have retired from your job, you can still contact the human resource department or the financial firm managing your payments to learn more about the specifics of your account.

Other Retirement Vehicles

In the current marketplace, there is a good variety of ways to save for retirement. You are not limited to investing through your employer. You can even have more than one retirement account if you wish. As you consider writing your will, it becomes important for you to keep in mind where these funds are best invested so they can be used in retirement and later left for your heirs or other beneficiaries if you so choose. Bear in mind that most retirement plans will require a spousal waiver for early withdrawal of funds and designation of nonspousal beneficiaries.

The following sections describe some of the most common retirement options available. Some still have sponsorship through employers while others do not.

The 401(k) retirement plan

The 401(k) is a type of defined contribution retirement plan. It is one of the best choices for many people and is commonly used. In a 401(k), contributions come from your paycheck on a pretax basis, which means they are not subject to withholding because they are tax-deferred accounts. You will not make tax payments on these funds until after you begin to make withdrawals from your retirement plan during retirement.

Many employers will contribute to your 401(k) plan themselves. For example, they might match your contribution up to a certain percentage. If this is the case, be sure you are contributing enough to get the maximum employer match; your employer is giving you free money in your retirement plan as a fringe benefit. With retirement accounts, there is usually a date or age at which you can start pulling money from your account. There is also a date by which you must start pulling money from your account. With a 401(k) plan, you need to be at least 59 ½ years old to start taking money out of the fund without a tax penalty. You can delay using the funds until you reach 70 ½ years old. You can learn more at the Internal Revenue Service's website (**www.irs.gov**).

There is a version of a 401(k) called a SIMPLE plan designed to work in the same way, but the plan is used when the company has fewer than 100 employees. In the SIMPLE 401(k), the employer's contribution is limited to 3 percent, while it can be as much as 25 percent for a regular 401(k). Employer contributions are immediately vested in SIMPLE 401(k) plans, while they might be deferred on a vesting schedule in regular 401(k)s. Also, an employer who has a SIMPLE 401(k) is not permitted to have other plans in place; this limitation is not tied to a regular 401(k) plan.

Another form of employer retirement benefit plan is the 403(b) plan, designed for individuals who work in certain public sector jobs and the nonprofit industry. This type of plan functions similarly to the 401(k) plan for private employers. People with a 403(b) plan often confuse what they have as a 401(k) because of this similarity. Your plan description will explain what type of plan you have. If you work for a public employer or nonprofit organization, you likely have a 403(b).

Individual retirement accounts

An individual retirement account (IRA) is another form of retirement account you can set up personally with a financial institution. Although your employer generally manages the 401(k), you can set up an IRA anywhere you would like.

IRAs are similar in terms of structure to that of a 401(k). With an IRA, the money contributed to the plan is still tax deferred, which means you do not pay taxes on this money until you withdraw it. When the funds come out, taxes are assessed on the funds as regular income tax. The hope is you will be included in a lower tax bracket when you begin using the money.

A Roth IRA is a different story. In this type of retirement plan, you actually are investing after-tax dollars into the plan. For example, your income is taxed when you are paid through your employer. You then take some of the remaining money from your paycheck and deposit the funds into a Roth IRA. The funds have already been taxed so no taxes are assessed when you begin using the money. The benefit here is that the funds you have contributed will grow tax free throughout the investment period, and there is no tax to pay on any of those funds when you withdraw them.

You might have other types of retirement accounts and pension plans, or you might have nothing now. In both cases, you should be considering how your situation affects your will plan. With most forms of IRAs, you can list a pay-on-death (POD) beneficiary on the account. This person is able to collect any funds remaining in your accounts when you die.

For example, suppose you have invested wisely, and your 401(k) account contains more than $2 million at the time of your retirement. Because you do not need it right away, you do not start taking the funds out until you have to at age 70 ½. These funds are not likely to be in use during the remaining portion of your life unless you do some heavy spending. Therefore, chances are good there will be some funds remaining, and your beneficiary will receive these.

When writing your will, keep in mind who your beneficiary is. Will your friend James get all of your money, or will your son inherit it? As part of planning what will happen to your assets, keep these retirement accounts in mind for your will. If your son Sean will be getting the remains of your retirement account, you might want to list your daughter Sasha in your will as receiving other property.

You do not specifically need to list retirement accounts and beneficiaries in your will because the proceeds from such accounts will be conveyed to the beneficiary listed on the accounts.

As with any other portion of your assets, you should review your decisions regarding beneficiaries on these accounts and change them as needed. If you marry, have another child, or just change your mind, you can contact your human resource department or the investment firm directly to have this information updated.

CASE STUDY:
A LOVED ONE'S EXPERIENCE

Zelda Morgan
Dallas, Texas

Zelda Morgan had a good experience with her siblings and with the entire will and estate business when her mother died recently. She had been chosen as both sole executer and power of attorney for her mother before she died. Thrust into the situation, Morgan knew she and her mother had never had a problem talking about their wishes after death, and her siblings (there were two) did not try to override her or give her a hard time.

"Even though I was the youngest, my brother and sister knew my mother wanted me as her executor and power of attorney, and they didn't try to butt into me doing my job in those roles. Because we all got along, which is apparently not so common, I involved them every step of the way so we all three could feel like we were making the decisions together, and we really were."

Even before Morgan's mother died, she knew her mother did not want to be hooked up to a machine keeping her alive. Morgan also knew that someday she would have to be the one to make that call; when it happened, it was not what she expected.

Morgan's mother was 82 years old, so it was not uncommon for her to have to go to the hospital for various health reasons. On this day, she had been taken to the hospital and Morgan had been called to come there as her power of attorney. She found her mom in the emergency room, and the nurse in charge told her that her mother would be able to see her and would regain consciousness in about 30 minutes. Thirty minutes later, she was called to the ICU with her husband and brother and asked if her mother had wanted to be on life support.

"I had no idea what a life support machine even looked like before that day," Morgan recalled. "The doctor called me in the room and asked me if my mother wanted to be on life support. I asked him what he was talking about. Unfortunately, this doctor had the bedside manner of a baboon, and when I asked him if my mom would wake up, he shook his and said, 'Nope, she's out of it.' She was like a limp dishrag. After a few choice words with the doctor, we called the family and told them to come. Two hours later my mom died but with her siblings, children, and friends by her side."

Morgan's father had died in March of 2005, and it was at that time that her mother began preparing for what would happen in the event of her death. Fortunately, she had all the paperwork together and let her children know where the money was, how much there was, and any of the other details that would be necessary after she passed away. It was at this time that Morgan's mother also put her in charge.

"My brother and his wife also moved in with my mom; this way, she was able to live at home until she died. So my brother took care of the day-to-day, my sister handled any phone calls relating to insurance or business matters, and I made the overall bigger decisions. Everyone got to take part in my mother's last days," Morgan said.

When her mother died, Morgan had a copy of the will and most of the funeral expenses had been paid for already. Her mother had also paid all her bills off with the exception of one credit card, and she had supplemental insurance, leaving no hospital or medical bills that had to be paid.

"I have never heard of anyone doing it, and I can't believe how well my mother took care of matters before she died — she left us quite a bit of money and no problems," Morgan said. "I also think my siblings and I got along so well because we knew my parents would have been horrified if we had argued."

Chapter 6

Beneficiaries and Gifts

As noted, beneficiaries are people you list in your will to receive something. However, "who gets what" can be a tough decision for anyone writing a will. Some people might not feel like they own anything worth giving to anyone else, while others might want to find a way to leave more (or less) to one person as opposed to another. Only you can make these decisions.

In most situations, this can actually be a pleasant process because it allows you to think about taking care of someone important to you. Consider what your gift(s) will provide to that person.

Dividing Up Your Possessions

You can leave your belongings to friends and family in many ways. For example, you might choose to leave everything you own to your spouse. Alternatively, you might choose to divide all your belongings among several people. For example, you can leave all of your investments to your four children, in which each child gets a quarter of the stock you own. You can leave some or all of your assets to a charity. You can choose to give all your assets to a friend assuming you are not married. You might be interested in leaving your money to a school in the form of a scholarship for a specific category of student. The options are limitless if they are chosen with proper legal planning.

While listing your property and beneficiaries, you might start to wonder whether you can put a few restrictions in place in your will. You might want to attach some strings to your gifts. For example, you might decide you want your son to go to college, and therefore, you want to list in your will that he will not receive your monetary gift unless he does. People can attach many strings, but such strings are considered special circumstances and might not be honored by the court, depending on the type of will you intend.

Within your will, you might have specific goals you want to achieve, and these restrictions can make the process of probate longer. Should these restrictions not be possible, property could be tied up for years.

Life estates

An example of placing strings on your property is the life estate. With a life estate, you do not give the property entirely to the beneficiary. Rather, you give the beneficiary the right to use the property during his or her lifetime. Then, you name another individual to inherit the property — the remainder — after the lifetime holder dies. The life estate holder possesses a life interest, and the remainder owner has a legally enforceable future interest. If the remainder owner does not survive, the property becomes part of the remainder owner's estate unless an alternate remainder beneficiary has been named. There might be a tax benefit to this arrangement. This also ensures the property stays in the family. The best way to create such an arrangement is to create a trust that will put the property outside probate. The property rights will be enforced by the trustee according to the terms of the trust. If it is done through your will, the beneficiaries will have an enforceable claim to their respective interests in the property through the probate court.

For example, suppose you are wealthy, and your son and his wife are also financially stable. The family business is thriving and you know your son will not need your money. Instead of leaving your property to your son, you might wish to leave the property in a life estate so your son can use and take care of it, but he does not ultimately inherit it. Rather, your granddaughter will inherit it when her parents die. By doing this, the property is not subject to double taxes. If you did not do this, the property would face estate taxes at the time of your death and then again at the time of your son's death. Instead, it finds a place in this trust, which allows it to avoid such circumstances. Your son is the life estate beneficiary, and your granddaughter is the remainder interest beneficiary. You will need to speak to your attorney about establishing a plan like this.

Conditions, conditions

The life estate-remainder situation is an example of gifting property subject to certain restrictions. Another situation of restricted giving is conditional gifting. This type of gift comes with conditions that must be satisfied before the beneficiary is entitled to receive it free and clear. If the conditions are not satisfied, the gift remains in the estate or will go to another person. For example, assume you own a classic car collection that you wish to give to your daughter, but you want to make sure that she understands the importance of maintaining these cars before she takes possession of the collection. Your will can state that as a condition of receiving the cars, she must take a course of study in auto mechanics. If she does not do so, the gift instead will go to your nephew who is already familiar with cars.

Setting up such conditions can be difficult because there are many "what if" situations to consider. For example, in the above scenario, what happens if your daughter cannot afford to take the classes? Did you provide for the cost of the classes in your will? Or, suppose she is employed by then and cannot take time off from work? When does she have to enroll? What if she fails the course? Are there circumstances in which you would still want her to inherit the cars that will be foreclosed by your condition of taking this auto mechanics course? May she take the course online? Unforeseeable circumstances also could occur, but you will not be able to modify or eliminate your will's condition after you are gone.

Instead of a conditional gift like this, you might instead wish to leave behind a message in your explanatory letters outlining what your wishes are. Your beneficiaries will not be legally obligated to obey your wishes, but you can impress upon them why you would like them to do certain things.

Types of Beneficiaries

There are various types of beneficiaries, and before you start writing your will, consider their differences so you can make the best decisions for you. The more specific you are in your will, the better your goals will be met when the will is administered. The types of beneficiaries are:

- **Primary beneficiaries:** Primary beneficiaries are the individuals who are your first choice to receive your property. In most situations, the primary beneficiary simply will receive the item you have bequeathed to him or her. Examples can include leaving your son your stocks to a business, your wife your investment accounts, and your daughter your special collection of art pieces.

- **Equally shared beneficiaries:** There might be a time when you just cannot choose one person to receive the subject property. If you would like two or more people to share ownership of one item, this is an equally shared beneficiary. An example of this is leaving the family home to your daughter and your son, each having equal undivided ownership in the property.

- **Alternative or contingency beneficiaries:** What happens if your primary beneficiary predeceases you or refuses to accept the gift? In this case, the property would fall to your residuary beneficiary, or if the residue has no beneficiary, to intestate determination by the probate court. The fix is to list alternate, or contingent, beneficiaries for any item you list. For example, suppose you want to leave your coin collection to your son. You name his son (your grandson), as the alternative beneficiary in case your son predeceases you or refuses the gift. Naming your alternative beneficiaries is important. Simply list one or two people whom you wish to receive gifts that your primary beneficiary would have received. If you are leaving items to people older than you or in poor health, it is important to include alternatives because you could outlive them. You can change your will after their death, of course, but there is always a chance you could also die before you are able to change your will.

- **Residuary beneficiaries:** A residuary beneficiary is the person named to receive the balance of the estate after all specific gifts in the will have been satisfied. It is important to list this beneficiary in the will. Often, the "residue" is the bulk of the estate. The residuary beneficiary does not receive property that legally passes to someone else outside of your will, such as property that passes under a joint survivorship arrangement. You can provide for the residue to be divided among multiple beneficiaries by stating it in percentages. For example, if you name your two brothers as residuary beneficiaries, decide whether the property is to be split equally or if one person should receive more of the property than the other. You should also list an alternative residuary beneficiary. Like other alternates, this person is your backup plan. This person will receive property from your will if your primary residuary beneficiary dies before you do or refuses the bequest. Similarly, if you name two or more residuary beneficiaries, list an alternate for each of these individuals. Here is an excerpt from a sample will to illustrate: "I leave my residuary estate to my brother Joseph Smith. That is, the rest of my property not specifically listed in my will is to be left to my brother Joseph Smith. This will include lapsed or failed gifts in addition to others I fail to mention. If Joseph Smith dies prior to my death, I leave my entire residuary estate to my sister, Crystal Smith."

Survivorship Provisions

A will might have a clause in which a beneficiary must survive the testator by a specific amount of time in order to inherit the gift. This helps avoid complex situations in the deaths of multiple individuals. A survivorship period simply states that if your primary beneficiary dies within a defined period of time after your death, the primary beneficiary will not obtain your property, but rather, the property will revert to an alternative beneficiary. In doing this, you avoid the property being transferred twice and quickly diminished in successive probate proceedings. The first transfer would be from you to the primary beneficiary, and the second would be from that individual to his or her heir or beneficiary in turn. Consider the following example:

Jim states in his will that his brother, Allen, will receive $50,000 worth of investments when Jim dies. Jim also states that Allen must survive him by 30 days; if he does not, the $50,000 goes to Jim's nephew Justin. Unfortunately, after Jim dies, his brother also dies just three weeks later. Because Jim has put a 30-day survivorship period into his will, Allen does not receive his property. Instead, the money goes directly to Justin. Had Jim not done this, the $50,000 would have gone to Allen's estate and been subject to a second round of tax and costs there before final distribution to Allen's beneficiary, who might be someone Joe had no intention of benefitting. The $50,000 could be significantly reduced, and certainly held up in estate limbo by going through this process twice.

By including a survivorship clause, you also ensure your property does not fall under the control of someone else's will. To continue with the previous example, if Jim has left his estate to Allen, but Allen dies soon after, Jim's property goes to Allen's residuary beneficiary. Someone Jim might not know could acquire his money, a result Jim did not intend.

Most people include alternate beneficiaries in their wills; some omit them because they do not think of the possible outcome. It is necessary to think ahead to possible scenarios when drafting your will.

Comments Made to Beneficiaries in Wills

Adding comments to beneficiaries in a will might be important in some instances. As mentioned earlier, comments are phrases that express your wishes or explain your remarks left in a will. Generally, comments are best placed in an explanatory letter accompanying your will. However, there are times when you might want to include these comments in the will itself.

Whenever there is a need to explain a gift clearly, consider including a comment in the will. Such explanations can serve to help your wishes be understood if a question arises. For example, you might leave a prized possession to someone who has helped you throughout your life. Your comment might be, "To my dear friend Liz Amos, I leave my prized brooch collection in appreciation for all the help and guidance she has provided throughout my life." Or, another example might be, "To Doctor Pat Elliot, I leave $50,000 for all the hard work he has done in support of my pets."

Some attorneys might want you to leave out all comments from a will. The thinking behind this is that comments left in a will, even short and simple ones, can be confusing. They might be misleading if not written properly. If you do want to leave comments to beneficiaries, you can as long as you do so properly. Be sure the words you use cannot be construed in a way that would alter the substance of the will in a way you did not intend or raise a question about your mental capacity.

Types of gifts

There are various ways to provide and include gifts in the will. Make sure to include specifics in this portion of the will.

Debt forgiveness

A more unique gift to give to an individual is debt forgiveness. Within the will, you can itemize a debt you wish to forgive from a person by simply declaring it forgiven and stating the person is not required to pay it back to the estate. Someone else must owe the debt to you. By forgiving a debt, you release the individual from any and all obligation to repay that debt. Both written and oral debts can be forgiven in this way. If you do not forgive the debt, your executor has the obligation to collect it on behalf of the estate.

If you are married and wish to forgive a debt, both spouses must agree on the transaction. Depending on whether you live in a common law or a community property law state, your spouse might have a right to claim that debt. You might wish to explain your debt forgiveness in your explanatory letter. For example, if you forgive a business partner from repaying an investment, explain why you did this.

Shared gifts

Are there items you wish to leave to more than one person? Shared gifts are legal. A common example of this is leaving specifically named property behind to children. You might want your children to share your home, for example. There are some complications that can arise out of this situation, though. You need to take steps to ensure your wishes will, and can, be carried out.

A common complication arises when not all of the recipients of the property wish to keep it and some wish to split the proceeds from the sale as defined. You might have a dream of your three children enjoying the house on the lake with their children, but they might have other ideas or be unable to agree about when to use it, how to maintain it, and whether guests can use it. A similar complication is the refusal of one to pay his or her share of maintenance of the property.

Whenever there is a disagreement with how a property is to be managed, the recipients must work out a solution on their own. More so, they must determine the best route for moving forward legally. Often, situations that are unable to be resolved can end up in court for a judge or jury to decide. Legally, your will only holds enough power to give the property to these recipients unless you have include stipulations with the gift. For example, if they fail to get along, it shall be donated to your church. What is done with the property after this point is out of your hands unless the property is placed in a trust with a trustee managing it.

One example of a step you can take to avoid such conflicts is putting stipulations in your will to govern the property. For example, you can list that the property may not be sold unless all of the recipients agree it should be sold. Keep in mind that this can aggravate a situation. If you have three children and two of them wish to sell and one does not, under this condition of unanimous agreement, the property cannot be sold. Who is financially responsible for maintaining the property? What if one of the three wishes to live in the property, but the other two do not want this to happen?

One solution to shared gifts is to work out an agreement prior to your death. You can use your explanatory letter to share your views or reaffirm such decisions in conjunction with the will's provisions. Nevertheless, it should be a discussion you have with your family when you are drawing up your will. If you do make decisions regarding property such as this, be sure everyone comes to an agreement to ensure children are not left to question decisions.

Even so, remember that people change their minds or their circumstances change. Many testators have created a legacy of wrangling and bitterness quite unintentionally. The best approach is to build in a means to resolve a dispute should it arise. You might wish your three children happily share the vacation cottage on the lake, but if they cannot agree or cannot maintain it together equally, it is better for you to decide how it should be sold — or which of them gets it or whether it should be donated to charity — than for them to be fighting over it.

When listing shared gifts in your will, be sure to state the percentage of ownership. Ownership can be labeled as equally shared or shared by a specific percentage. For example, you might wish to leave your home equally to each of your three children. You would then write in your will, "I leave my home at (address) equally to my children Maria Martinez, Ava Martinez, and Daniel Martinez." On the other hand, you might wish one child to receive more ownership, so in this case you would write, "I leave my home at (address) to my children jointly as follows: 50 percent to Maria Martinez, 25 percent to Ava Martinez, and 25 percent to Daniel Martinez."

Real estate can also be set up to pass by joint survivorship deed outside of your will. There are few options for conditions of ownership using this mechanism, however. If you want to set up joint ownership of a property with conditions of use and options for resolving disputes, placing it in a trust or setting up the arrangement through your will is a better choice. Similar considerations apply to such shared gifts as boats and RVs.

Gifts for one person

For those who are leaving gifts in their will to one person, the process of naming an alternative beneficiary is relatively easy. You simply list the gifts by name, the name of the primary beneficiary, and the name of the alternative beneficiary. An example of this would be written as, "I leave my art collection of ten Impressionist oil paintings to my cousin Jules Abel. If Jules does not survive me, then I leave this art collection to my cousin James Lue."

There are no rules restricting who you name as your alternative beneficiaries. At the same time, be as descriptive as possible in identifying these gifts and naming the individual you leave them to. Also, if you are naming two beneficiaries to share the same gift as alternatives, list this clearly and the amount of ownership each one has. For example, in this scenario, you would write, "I leave my art collection of ten Impressionist oil paintings to my cousin Jules Abel. If Jules does not survive me, I leave this art collection to my cousins James Lue and Susie Lue to share equally."

Gifts for shared recipients

If you are listing shared gifts in your will, it is important to list alternatives. This could be confusing, especially when unequal portions of the property are distributed. If you decide to leave property to two or more people and one of those people does not survive you, list an alternative to take his or her place in the same equation. For example, if you are leaving property to two people and you want them both to equally share in the property, list an alternative for each half share.

Instead of providing an alternative for a beneficiary receiving a shared gift, you can provide that if one of the shared beneficiaries dies, the remaining beneficiary takes the entire gift. This eliminates the need for an alternative beneficiary. For example, if you are splitting property between two people and one of them dies prior to your death, you might wish for the other named individual to receive the full rights to the property. These items need to be spelled out in the will as such.

How many layers of alternatives do you need? In either shared gifts or in gifts to one person, it is best to list at least one alternative. It is rare to need additional layers, but if you feel the need to do so, you can list as many as wish. Work with an attorney to get your alternatives listed clearly according to your intent.

Splitting by percentage

It might be necessary to split most of your assets among a small group of people. This is also a common way to delineate a testamentary gift. For example, you might state you want all of your property to be equally divided among your three children, listing them by name. If you do not want an equal split, however, you can describe their inheritance in terms of percentage instead.

For example, your son Kevin receives 30 percent of your property, while your daughter Jamie receives 70 percent. When all of your property is divided like this, there is no need to list out property rights to specific items unless you want specific individuals to own these items. Then, this format will not work for you. It is essential for you to realize that in situations of percentages, it might be necessary for your executor to sell the property and split the proceeds among the beneficiaries according to the percentages you have outlined. Also, even if you are sure you have accounted for all your property by the percentage split, you should still include a residuary clause to be sure 100 percent of your property is accounted for by your will.

Specific bequests

Many people want to leave special items to special people. Leaving individual gifts to primary beneficiaries is an option in any will. Identify the individual by name and relationship to you, and list the specific property he or she is to receive. It is essential to clearly identify the specific property of your bequest and the person who is to receive it. The property must be described well enough to be understood by someone who does not know the person or the item. For example, if you own only one grand piano and you wish to leave it to your only daughter, Ann Smith, it might be sufficient to simply state, "I leave my grand piano to my daughter Ann Smith."

Contrast that with the following example. Assume you own a large number of antique clocks and you want to leave specific clocks to specific people. In this situation, you will need to identify each clock in a manner that makes it clear which clock you intend to leave to each specific person. It might not be enough to describe the clocks by physical characteristics or location if they are similar in appearance and are all located in your house. In such a case, you might consider labeling each clock with a serial number and including that number in your bequest in your will. Keeping labeled clear photographs of the clocks and other items with your will to illustrate bequests can also be helpful. If you have a number of items to bequeath in your will that might cause any possible confusion, work with your attorney to be sure the will is as clear as possible.

Including your children in your will

You can include your children in the will with specifics. Try to avoid fighting and favoritism here. Again, explanatory letters can be useful to foreclose possible misunderstandings or questions about your decisions.

Identify all children

When leaving property to your children, list them by name. If you should list that your property is to be equally shared by "my children" this implies that all children are equal. What about adopted children? Perhaps you have a child with an ex-spouse with whom you have little contact. All will be included within the term "my children" because it has legal significance.

Most state laws recognize adopted children the same as natural-born children. For children born out of wedlock, the rules are a bit less structured. From the standpoint of the mother, children born out of wedlock are presumed to be the actual child of the woman and are therefore permitted to receive property. From the standpoint of the father, there is a presumption that children born out of wedlock are not actually the father's child unless the father has legally acknowledged them. One way that the father might have legally acknowledged a child as his own might be to have paid child support for the child in the past or admitted in court that he was the father of the child. Paternity tests can resolve this issue as well.

Suppose you want to disinherit a child for some reason. Perhaps you have already paid out money to that child during your lifetime. State this in your will rather than simply omitting any reference to this child. This forecloses the child's opportunity to contest the will as a "forgotten" beneficiary.

All states give children equal inheritance rights if born posthumously but conceived while the deceased parent was still alive.

Posthumously conceived children

What about a child conceived after a parent has died? Medical advances, such as using frozen embryos and frozen sperm, offer individuals more options. Individuals conceived after one of their parent's death are uniquely viewed in terms of estate law. Unfortunately, there is little guidance about all possible situations, as this is a relatively new advent to estate proceedings. The birth of a child after the death of a parent might occur for several reasons, but one situation that has recently presented interesting questions concerning the rights of the child is the birth of a child from frozen sperm where the father dies prior to the conception. Does this child qualify for part of the father's estate? Similarly, is the child eligible for governmental death benefits?

Some states have ruled that posthumous children conceived in this way do qualify for the same benefits as children born prior to the death of their parent. Other states have ruled that they do not. In 2002, the Massachusetts Supreme Court held in *Woodward v. Commissioner of Social Security* that two children conceived by in vitro fertilization with a deceased husband's sperm have the right to inherit from the man's estate as long as the mother could establish that her husband consented to the posthumous conception and would have agreed to support any resulting children.

Many states outline the rules related to children conceived posthumously in state statutes. For example, California's Probate Code provides that a posthumous child may inherit from the deceased parent if all of the following conditions are met:

1. The parent must leave behind a written document stating his or her wishes for his or her genetic material to be used to conceive a child even after they die.

2. The only person able to use this material is the deceased person's spouse, a registered domestic partner, or someone else named specifically in the will.

3. This document must be filed with the executor of the will at least four months prior to the death of the parent. Written documentation must be given to the will's executor that states the genetic material has been made available and who is able to receive it.

4. Finally, the conception of the child must occur within two years of the parent's death.

These laws are complicated, and they often are designed this way to avoid abuses of the law. It is also important to note that these laws are still new and are changing. Therefore, if you know you are likely to die in a matter of months and would like to give your spouse this benefit, do so in writing with assistance of an attorney. Your state's laws will need to be followed closely to allow for the child to receive all legal rights as your lawful offspring. *A list of each state's current law about inheritance rights of posthumously conceived children can be found in Appendix B.*

Disabled children

Do you have a disabled child? Be careful when leaving behind any real property or other assets to this individual. Although your intentions might be good, it might cause a financial problem for him or her, especially if the individual qualifies for social programs offered by the government. For example, if you leave your property to your disabled son, this will increase his financial net worth. Having a higher net worth might disqualify him from eligibility for government assistance programs from which he now benefits. An alternative option for such a situation is to create a trust to benefit this child and appoint a trustee who will in turn use the trust's funds for his benefit. Of course, the trustee must be someone in whom you are confident to handle the responsibility with dedication to your child's best interests.

Before making any decisions regarding creating such an arrangement or something similar, consult your attorney. The decision should be based on the type of property, the amount of property, the type of disability and needs of the child, and the goals you have for your child.

Your Beneficiaries

Selecting your beneficiaries and how you will leave them is rarely a snap decision. How you look at these questions will likely change over time. Your perspective and goals while children are young will be focused primarily on their ongoing welfare. As you grow older and they become independent, unless a disability is involved, you might have a different view of how your assets should be distributed when you are gone. Your own circumstances might change in terms of how much you own.

When you make your will, do so for what you currently need. You will modify it from time to time, as these circumstances change in ways that affect your estate planning.

Leaving property to minor children or young adults

Leaving property to minors is possible. In most states, a minor is legally defined as an individual under the age of 18. In some, the age can be 21. Should you wish to leave something to them, you must also list an adult to manage the property. Otherwise, it will likely fall into the hands of a parent to manage or someone appointed by the court instead. Minors are able to own property, and they can be willed property, yet a representative must be in charge of the property until the child reaches the age of majority.

A young adult is someone who is no longer a minor but who is still sufficiently young enough that you may wish to protect the property he or she receives until older. You might want to place property in a trust until the young person reaches a specific age. For example, he or she may not inherit the property that makes up a trust fund until reaching age 30, Legally, this is possible to do. In this case, the trustee monitors, oversees, and/or invests the property until the child reaches the designated age.

Leaving property to an organization

A legal organization, such as a corporation, can be designated as beneficiary in a will. Tax-exempt charities and even labor unions can receive such property. Both public and private organizations are legally able to receive your property. To arrange for such gifts in a will, simply list the specific organization by its legal name and address and describe the property you wish it to receive.

Leaving property to out of country individuals

Many people have family members who live out of the country. It is acceptable to leave your property to someone living abroad. In fact, as long as you list the beneficiary's legal name, there is no limitation. It will be the duty of your executor to find this person and award him or her the gift. Do make it easy on your executor, though. Leave information about how to locate this beneficiary. If you do not know how to do so, set a time period for the executor to succeed in locating the person, with an alternate to take the property instead if the primary beneficiary cannot be found.

On the other hand, if you own property outside the United States, you must abide by the laws of that country when leaving property behind. For example, if you own a home and real estate in Italy, your will, which was drafted in the United States, might not be enough. You might also need to have a will on file with an attorney in Italy outlining your goals for that property.

Disinheritance: Saying No

Imagine a person in your life whom you simply cannot tolerate. Perhaps there is someone in your close family with whom you no longer have contact. You might feel strongly about avoiding any inheritance reaching this person.

What is disinheritance? Most people writing a will have no use for disinheriting because they are outlining their wishes fairly specifically. Yet, it could happen that you intend to disinherit someone. The term simply means you are ensuring someone who might otherwise inherit from you will be excluded from your estate.

You can, in most situations, disinherit anyone from your will except for your spouse, according to the state's mandatory spousal portion. In the state of Florida, for example, you are required to leave your home to your spouse if you have minor children. Also, if you have a contract written before you die that requires you leave property to a specific person, you cannot override the contractual obligation by your will.

Using a no-contest clause

Perhaps you want to be sure the person you list in your will actually gets your bequest. To do this, you can include a no-contest clause in the will. This clause states that anyone who challenges the will and fails to win that challenge is automatically removed from the will and is no longer able to receive anything from the will. Why would you want to do this? If you want to be sure no one challenges your will, this can be one of the best ways to do so. Anyone who challenges the will risks losing anything you did leave to that person. A no-contest clause is often added to a will to discourage beneficiaries from fighting among themselves in the probate courts. Work out this type of language with assistance of legal counsel.

When the Property is not There

Having organized the disposition of all your property to selected beneficiaries, one other future contingency is if your ownership of bequeathed property changes. Keep in mind that a will is not binding while you are alive. You are not limited as to what you do with your property simply because you have accounted for it in your will. Property can be bought, sold, given way, lost, stolen, or destroyed.

Perhaps you have bequeathed your favorite coin collection to someone in your will. If you have sold that collection by the time of your death, the person you named to receive it no longer is able to get it. This is called ademption. Depending on state law, the beneficiary might not be entitled to equivalent funds in the will instead of the coin collection. Other states will not allow the beneficiary to receive anything; they consider the gift lapsed because it no longer exists. One way to keep this situation in hand for yourself is to include a provision in your will that covers the topic of ademption. You can decided how you want adeemed gifts to be handle, in case you have not had time to update a will that contains an adeemed gift.

There is also the case of insufficient funds to pay out the gifts to all your beneficiaries. This is situation is called abatement. If the testator writes out specific rules on how $250,000 will be distributed among family members, but there is only $200,000 at the time of death, obviously not enough money is available to fulfill all of the requirements. Although the testator will not always know precisely the amount of a possible shortfall, he or she can still provide instructions as to which bequests should be used first to satisfy debt (or all of them according to a stated proportion). Consider it a "plan B" contingency. If the testator does not write directions in the event of insufficient funds, the decision will fall under the state's probate law to determine the answer.

Generally, state law covers abatement by first satisfying any specific gifts of property named in the will. If the sewing machine was left to Sally, this will be given to Sally. If the antique bottles were left to Sam, these will be given to Sam. Second, general gifts are satisfied ($10,000 to Grace) if possible. The residuary of the estate (the remaining assets that were not specifically gifted) are sold and the funds are then used toward the amount listed in the will. Assuming there is not enough money left from the residuary liquidation, general gifts are invaded on a pro rata basis to satisfy the will's shortfall. For example, if two general beneficiaries were to each receive $100,000 of a $200,000 investment fund and there is only $80,000 left in the fund at time of death, each would get 50 percent ($40,000) of the funds available, the equivalent proportion of the fund as originally bequeathed to them.

Because these rules vary by state, it is important to understand how they will affect your will. One of the best ways to avoid having to deal with this situation is to leave percentages in your will rather than specific dollar amounts as well as instructions about how abatement shall be handled if necessary. Instead of listing the $200,000 in the example above, simply state that each beneficiary is to receive 50 percent of the proceeds in the investment fund.

Avoiding these types of problems is one of several reasons to update your will from time to time. In most cases, you will want to update cash items listed in your will at least one time per year or more often if needed. This helps to avoid any large differences found in the will at the time of your death.

Make Decisions

Integral to planning your will is identifying your desired beneficiaries and matching them with your intended gifts. Work through your list of beneficiaries and be sure all of your important gifts are included. It is important to make decisions regarding your property that you own up to this point in your life. In other words, if you hope you will have more assets or funds, do not include that in your plan for this moment. Rather, write a will that gives beneficiaries what you have right now. By doing so, should something happen to you right now, your wishes can be fulfilled. Down the road, as circumstances change, you can come back to your decisions and change them to better suit your life at that point.

Once you have worked through this aspect of your will, you should have a list of property and beneficiaries. Then, include alternative beneficiaries, your residuary beneficiary, and your alternative residuary beneficiary in a list. Soon, you will be able to put this together into your will's document. Before you can do that, though, you need to name a few more people, including the most important person of all within your will: your executor.

Chapter 7

The Executor

As you begin to write your will, you must decide who will be best suited to handle your estate. As you know, the executor (or executrix) is the individual you name to probate your will, manage the matters of your estate, and ensure your wishes are followed. This person is responsible for locating the will, safeguarding all of your property, filing appropriate documents with the court, locating beneficiaries, notifying and satisfying creditors, and following the directives in the will. Because this job is so important, it is critical that you select the best person for the responsibility. With married couples, the executor is often the surviving spouse, but this is not required, nor always the case. Some estates include co-executors, as did President John F. Kennedy. President Kennedy's will, made in Washington D.C. in 1954, included the following clause appointing his executors:

"I hereby nominate, constitute and appoint my wife, JACQUELINE B. KENNEDY, and my brothers, ROBERT F. KENNEDY and EDWARD M. KENNEDY, as Executors of, and

Trustees under, this my Last Will and Testament; and if for any reason at any time any one of them does not qualify or is unable or unwilling to serve as such Executor or as such Trustee, I hereby nominate, constitute and appoint the following, in the order named, as Executrix or Trustee of this my Last Will and Testament (as the case may be) to fill any such vacancy: my sisters, EUNICE K. SHRIVER, PATRICIA LAWFORD and JEAN KENNEDY."

President Kennedy took the precaution of naming backup executrixes — his sisters. He refers to the executors as also trustees because of trust provisions provided in his will.

Are you planning not to name an executor? Perhaps you pass away prior to naming one. In either situation, if a will does not have an executor, probate court will assign one to the case as administrator or conservator of the estate. The terminology that applies depends on the state. The duties are the same. This person will administrate your will.

Probate

Probate court conducts the legal process of implementing wills. In this process, a judge verifies whether a will has been legally established. The court will ensure an estate is administered according to the specifications of the will. There are ways to avoid probate all together, such as with a trust and pay-on-death transfers of financial accounts, vehicles, and survivorship deeds of real estate. Overall, probate court can be to your advantage if you have many specific bequests because probate ensures your property receives even distribution to those who deserve it.

Having a will means that probate court has a more hands-off approach to your estate. After establishing its validity and legality, the court will simply oversee that your will is carried out according to your wishes. The court will not make decisions that do not coincide with your will, unless it includes unenforceable stipulations or does not follow the law of the state. For example, the court will ensure your physical assets are distributed the way you have them outlined in your will. Should an individual have a claim against your will, the probate court decides the validity of the claim.

However, if your will is exempt from going through formal probate, as is the case for smaller estates in some states, the executor of your will still ensures its provisions are executed. This means one person, solely, is responsible for making your will come to reality. Although family members can contest the process or the handling by the executor, this rarely happens. For this reason, it is important for you to select the right executor for your will and ensure he or she is capable of handling your property for you in the way you planned. You should provide a backup executor as well.

Directing Your Executor

Before you name someone to this important position, you should know what the person would be responsible for doing. Verify the individual you have chosen is willing and able to do the job. Because the task could be complex and require a legal hearing in probate court, appoint someone who can definitely understand the process, work well with an attorney, and fulfill the requirements of the court.

An executor's job can be complex. Each state provides for the exact responsibilities of the executor, and these differ from state to state. Some states even require the executor to be represented by a lawyer because knowledge of the process is beneficial. Most will templates have specific clauses in them that outline the responsibilities of the executor. Generally, these clauses will grant the executors extensive legal power for your estate. If you have purchased a will template or plan to use any premade form, read the executor's clause.

The following is a closer look at what most wills will include in terms of the responsibilities of the executor:

"I nominate _____ to be my executor and to carry out all legally permissible actions included in my will. I grant the executor the following powers so that he can execute my will in the best intentions of my estate.

- To pay my debts, including taxes, as the executor sees best, including taxations against my estate.

- To retain property without any liability to any loss or loss of value of said property.

- To sell any of my property, through private or public sale, as deemed necessary by my executor so that the funds may be in use as my will dictates or as my executor sees necessary.

- To vote stock; to sell bonds, stocks, and other financial investments in my name; to purchase other stocks as needed; to carry out the functions in my will; and to have the same privileges as someone who owns securities in his or her own right.

- To lease any property as needed, including any property that is part of my estate.

- To handle legal matters associated with my property including abandoning, compromise, sue on, defend, adjust or arbitrate, or otherwise handle problems in the favor of my estate.

- To become a participant in my business to continue, operate, maintain, or participate in the business as required to for incorporation, dissolution, or to make changes to the organization of the business.

- To handle all other acts, as deemed necessary; to manage my property; and to carry out the wishes in my will, including my investments, real property, and personal property."

Walt Disney's will, made under the laws of California, directed the will's co-executors (his wife and a bank) in the following language:

"Such Co-Executors shall have full power and authority to lease, sell, exchange or encumber the whole or any part of my estate, without notice, but subject to such confirmation as may be required by law and may continue to hold, manage and operate any property, and, subject to court approval, any business belonging to my estate. I further authorize and empower my Co-Executors, upon any division of my estate, or upon any partial or final distribution of my estate, to partition, allot and distribute my estate in undivided interests or in kind or partly in money and partly in kind according to such method or procedure as my Co-Executors shall determine; provided however, that in making an allocation of assets to the various trusts created under the provision of Article FIFTH above, any shares of stock of Retlaw Enterprises, Inc., or any successor corporation, or any interest in residential real properties which are included in the residue of my estate shall only be allocated to the Disney Family Trust provided for thereunder."

As you can see, there is a great deal of responsibility in the hands of the executor. The good news is the executor might not have to perform all of the duties mentioned above, but including them specifically is a precaution to prevent any possible problems arising after your death. The will is written with the executor's expressed rights to ensure if a bank or other organization comes forward and states they want to check the validity of a certain clause, the will is able to provide this information. It makes the executor's job easier.

In most situations, the assigned attorney will effectively manage a will, which goes to probate court, legally. For example, should the executor need to step into any of the above listed roles, such a taking control of a business, the probate attorney can handle the legalities. The probate attorney will also handle issues with investments so the executor has the legal right and ability to sell them, change them, or otherwise deal with them.

Usually, the probate attorney handles the majority of legal aspects. The executor will only need to sign legal papers prepared by the attorney and pay final taxes and other obligations as determined by your will, using the funds from the estate. More so, the executor is responsible for making sure personal property goes to those who have legal right to it. For example, if you leave in your will that you would like all of your clothing to go to a charity, the executor needs to take your clothing to the charity.

Executors' General Duties

The executor of your will is responsible for a variety of tasks, and these tasks begin soon after your death. Some of the duties your executor will be immediately responsible for and will likely deal with in the months after your death include:

- **Obtaining a copy of your will.** Tell your executor where your will is located or give him or her a copy to expedite the process. The executor is also responsible for locating a missing will.

- **Obtaining certified copies of your death certificate.** No transfer of property can take place unless a death certificate is presented. For example, your bank will require a certified copy of the death certificate to agree to liquidate the funds from the account so they can have funding as directed in your will. The executor of the will needs to locate all beneficiaries listed in the will. They should be given this contact information either prior to the process or as an accompaniment to the will.

- **Getting your affairs in order.** This includes:

  o Locating all of your property, in particular, property listed in the will.

  o Obtaining all records that prove ownership of property, such as deeds, bank statements, insurance policies, tax returns, and other documents.

  o Accessing your safety deposit box and taking inventory of what is there. An executor is not able to remove items from the box until probate approves the process (if the will goes through probate).

- **Carrying out the duties of managing your finances and property.** He or she will be immediately responsible for collecting and reading your mail, calling each of your credit card accounts and canceling the cards, canceling any other memberships you have (including things like magazine subscriptions and newspapers), and calling the Social Security Administration and other retirement accounts you have to stop payments or collect any payments due to you at that time.

- **Closing bank accounts and investment accounts.** The funds from the accounts might need to be transferred or liquidated, as specified in the will or by the probate court so the funds can move to the appropriate person at the end of the probate process.

- **Hiring an attorney.** If need arises, the executor has the right and ability to do this on behalf of your estate. For example, should someone contest the will, it is the executor's responsibility to hire a probate attorney to handle the court filings. Note, probate court will place a probate attorney in charge of your case, but this attorney is working for the court system, not for the estate. A probate attorney hired by your executor will fight for the estate.

- **Handling legal documents.** As your will works through probate or your estate is liquidated, the job of the executor continues. Because they are the legal authority on your estate, he or she is required to handle all legal documents him or herself, even if there is a spouse involved.

- **Managing and maintaining your property.** During the time your estate is going through probate or your estate is being liquidated, which could take a year or more depending on probate requirements, the executor of your will needs to manage and maintain your property. They need to pay taxes on real estate, pay utilities, and manage the upkeep of the property. These bills can be paid out from your estate, but records need to be kept of bills received and money paid out. Even personal property that has yet to be disposed of needs maintaining by the executor.

- **Transferring assets to beneficiaries.** When transferring property, the executor of the will needs to ensure the process happens legally. For example, simply turning over the keys to your home to your son is not enough. The executor must ensure the title of the home transfers properly. The same goes for any type of financial or investment accounts.

Probate courts are a check on your executor because of statutory requirements the courts must enforce, paperwork that must be filed with the court, and the instructions provided in your will. For instance, if your will dictates that property is to be sold and your executor sold it for a low price to himself, the court or one of your beneficiaries could take legal action against the executor. Here, the goal is to ensure the executor is not selling for an undermarket rate or otherwise taking advantage of his or her fiduciary position. An executor has a fiduciary responsibility to execute your estate as desired, which means he or she has the authority and duty to administer or hold your assets for your beneficiaries as specified. Of course, many of these duties will include financial decisions made on behalf of the estate.

What Does the Executor Get?

The executor of your will might also be a beneficiary of it, but this is not always necessary. For all of his or her hard work, what does the executor get? Each state has put in place a procedure for the executor to be paid a fee from the estate. This is a set amount the executor is entitled to for his or her duties. These fees are calculated differently in each state. In some states, a specific percentage of the estate's value is paid to the executor. In other states, a set fee is paid.

Most executors will waive this fee, usually because they are receiving some or all of the property from the estate anyway, and therefore, there is no need to receive the fee. As you work on your will, be sure to meet with and work with your executor on this topic. Find out what he or she would like you to arrange, if you can do so.

Alternatively, many testators provide that the executor shall serve without being paid a fee. This is a decision the executor has to make, and some people might not want the job. If the executor is also a substantial beneficiary, though, such as a spouse, there is no need for the executor to be also paid a fee. This is a decision you should make with assistance of legal counsel.

Is Bonding Necessary?

Another consideration when writing your will is whether it is necessary to bond the executor, which means the executor is required to purchase insurance to protect the beneficiary's property. Some probate courts can require this if they feel there is some risk that the executor is not going to execute his or her duties of good faith and fair dealing or if there is a risk that the executor might commit fraud against the estate. If you feel this way about your executor, reconsider giving that person the responsibility of being executor. It is also possible that beneficiaries would like to have this put in place. For the beneficiary, the protection comes in the form of protecting them from abuses by the executor for what they are entitled.

As the will writer, you can include a clause that waives the necessity of the executor being bonded. If you do not do so, or you wish for the executor to acquire a bond, the cost of the insurance protection (in the form of a bond) must come from the estate's value. The costs range widely, but on average, they are about 10 percent of the value of the estate. That is a steep payment to come out of the estate's value. Therefore, should you want this to be the case, realize that those funds will be cutting into the value of your estate that you leave behind to your beneficiaries.

Why would you want to have this type of bond in place? One reason is you might not have anyone you fully trust to name as executor. There might be a real risk that this person is not going to be honest. In this case, you can ensure he or she will uphold the duties properly by requiring the purchase of the bond.

In either situation, you should leave a clause in your will outlining your desire for the bond or your request that no bond be put in place. If you do not do this, probate court might require it of your executor.

Choosing the Best Executor

Choosing an executor is a serious decision. You need a person you trust fully to act as your executor. However, there is more to selecting an individual than just trust. For many people, the choice is obvious: a spouse. For others, it may be a child who is an adult. Still, your personal circumstances can dictate something else.

Most often, the person selected as executor is a spouse or close family member because that individual is someone who cares about the well-being of the property. For example, if you are assigning your son as your executor, he likely wants to ensure the property is well maintained and that your wishes are carried out. The executor often will receive the most from your will.

One of the first considerations you should have is the location of your executor. For both convenience of the state and the executor, select someone who lives in reasonable proximity to the court where your will is to be probated. An executor can be more remote if a local attorney is retained to most of the estate work, but it is not the ideal situation. Nevertheless, your trust and comfort with your nomination of executor are the overriding considerations. Geography is secondary to your certainty that you have left your will in good hands.

It is also important to talk to the executor before appointing this job. He or she must be willing to be your executor. Some people will not want such a responsibility or might feel they cannot do the job effectively on your behalf. If you name someone the executor of your will and he or she does not want this responsibility, he or she can turn down the job, allowing the alternative executor to step in.

Like all aspects of your will, it is important to come back and revise the executor's position if your circumstances change or your executor dies. At any time before your death, you can make changes to the executor by making a codicil to your will.

A question that is often brought up is making a decision between two people to be executor. If you cannot decide whom you will name executor, you can name more than one person, as you saw in the will clauses of President Kennedy and Walt Disney.

In the case of two executors, it is wise to make their respective responsibilities clear and provide for resolution of any difference of opinion should they have one on estate management. Three executors are capable of forming a majority on such matters, unless you have placed a requirement they agree unanimously, which can be a tall order. Watch your motivations here. Putting in place something like this will slow down the probate process, especially if one or more of those individuals is not readily accessible. If they cannot agree on a solution, what will happen? This is something you need to consider prior to assigning more than one person to be your executor with full authority.

The most common time this happens is when parents wish to name all of their children as equal executors in their will to help avoid any conflicts caused by hurt feelings. It might seem like a grand gesture, but in the long term, it can be limiting if the parties cannot agree. Ask your children who they feel should have the most responsibility. One of your children might be the obvious choice; for example, if your daughter is a lawyer who lives in your county, the others would understand choosing her as executor. For parents who know their children are capable of acting in unison, this might work just fine. Reality indicates, however, that nothing divides a family like an estate. In this case, a clause is added to the will that any one of the executors can make decisions on behalf of the estate. This alleviates such problems such as when one of the executors is not readily available.

As with your beneficiaries, when nominating an executor in your will, you need to also assign an alternative executor. President John F. Kennedy lined up his three sisters as alternates. This person takes over the duties as executor when the primary executor is unable or refuses to do so. This usually only happens if the primary executor dies or becomes ill prior to you and you have not made a formal change to your will.

Once again, such considerations underscore the importance of getting the assistance of experienced legal counsel for finalizing your will and estate plan.

CASE STUDY:
TIPS FROM A PROBATE JUDGE

Joseph Ashmore, Jr.
Law Offices of Joseph E. Ashmore,
Jr. P.C.
Dallas, Texas
www.ashmorelaw.com

Joseph Ashmore, Jr., a retired probate judge who served on the bench from 1975 to 1986, founded the Law Offices of Joseph E. Ashmore, Jr. P.C. in June of 1987. He has been working in wills and probate for over 30 years and is currently an attorney practicing in Dallas, Texas.

Although he has a lot to say about wills and estate, he noted one thing that many people do seem to forget: "I tell my clients that the most important thing to remember is that your will is about what you want and not what your family members might want. Inheritance is a privilege; it is not a right."

In regards to defining the difference between a will, a trust, and an overall estate plan, Judge Ashmore said, "An estate plan generally refers to all of the documents prepared for an individual and can include a will, trust, and other related documents. A will refers to a last will and testament. This document sets out the wishes of a testator to be enacted upon his or her death. Finally, a trust is a document that can be put in place for a variety of purposes prior to death and/or after death."

Judge Ashmore said it truly is important for a person have a will so his or her wishes are met upon death. He said, "In Texas, it is also much less expensive to probate a will than it is to seek an administration." Depending on the complexity of a will, often the person making it must have some help. That decision, however, depends on many things.

"This depends upon the size of your estate," Judge Ashmore began. "You might only need an attorney, or you might need numerous attorneys as well as financial advisors, accountants, and so on."

When asked about the least a person should do in order to have a legal will he noted, "Leave a holographic will that meets the requirements in Texas or in the state you reside."

That said, a holographic will can be written by the individual, but Judge Ashmore noted, "There are certain requirements it must meet as well as procedures required by the court to have the will admitted to probate."

As for probate, something Judge Ashmore is very familiar with, he noted that not all cases require the will to go through probate. "This depends on what types of assets belong to the estate," he explained, "and how they can be transferred."

Judge Ashmore said, "A will sets out a person's wishes upon their death. A trust can be put into place at any time for a variety of reasons and purposes."

Chapter 8

Providing for Children by Will

You are planning to be with your children throughout their young lives and well into their adulthood. However, what if this is not what happens? This is one of those "what-if" situations you need to plan for. What if you are involved in a horrible accident and both you and the other parent dies? Who will care for your children, and what means will they have to do so?

You should make plans for two distinct areas. Parents who have minor children, or children under the age of 18, need to provide for those children in terms of legal guardianship and financial needs. Young adult considerations also should be considered. For example, if you have a child who is a young adult, usually considered someone under the age of 30, you might want to put special requirements into your will that protect his or her inheritance until maturity makes him or her better likely to handle it.

Guardianship of Your Children

"Guardian" is a legal term used to define the person, or people, responsible for caring for a child or an adult who is adjudged legally incompetent. The guardian of a minor child is responsible for ensuring the child has proper housing, food, education, and a healthy living environment. They assume the role of the parent. Another way of putting it is stating the guardian stands *in loco parentis* for the child — in the role of parent. The court must appoint a guardian to care for the children of deceased (or unfit) parents. In some states, such as New York, parents can select the guardian and arrange for his or her appointment to be filed at the appropriate time. Most states, though, look to the parents' suggestions in their wills, with the court making the final determination according to what is considered to be in the best interest of the child.

Thus, in your will, you can nominate a guardian for your minor children, and, as with other nominations, an alternative "backup" guardian. The court will review the selection you have made, and assuming there is no countervailing consideration, appoint this person as guardian.

Your children might have godparents. This designation is not legally binding under the law. Godparents are generally a religious or cultural set of parents responsible for ensuring the children are raised according to the parents' religion and customs. This is not the same procedure as the appointment of a legal guardian. If you wish for the godparents of the child to assume this guardianship role, it is essential to name them as guardians in the will.

If no guardian is named in a will, the court will determine who will serve as your children's guardians, typically close relatives. If no one can be found suitable, the children could enter into state foster care.

Each state has a protocol for selecting an individual to take over guardianship of a child left without parents. Usually, the first choice is a surviving parent. Otherwise, the courts will look to the person or people nominated in your will. If there is no such person listed, or if this person is unfit for some reason, the judge moves on to the second choice. If the children are older (usually age 12 to 14 or older), the judge might ask the children about their preference. This is only a request, of course, and the judge must first ensure the feasibility of such a request.

Finally, the judge will determine if any family member presents the best choice. This usually starts with grandparents of the children and then moves to the parent's siblings or the child's older brother or sister. Once the judge looks at all options available, they will then select the most appropriate person to be guardian over the child.

The following nomination of guardian clause comes from the New York last will and testament of musician John Lennon, full name John Winston Ono Lennon:

"I nominate, constitute and appoint my wife YOKO ONO, as the Guardian of the person and property of any children of the marriage who may survive me. In the event that she predeceases me, or for any reason she chooses not to act in that capacity, I nominate, constitute and appoint SAM GREEN to act in her place and stead."

Note that this clause nominates the same guardian for "person" and "property" of the children. This is necessary because there are two forms of guardianship. Guardian of the person is one who takes care of the child each day, makes sure the child goes to school, eats, sleeps properly, gets proper medical care, and has a social life, love, and companionship. A guardian of the property is responsible for taking care of the financial matters for the child. If there are separate guardians for the person and the property, the property guardian's role is to make sure the person guardian has sufficient funds for the care of the child and then otherwise conserves, invests, and manages the child's financial matters. Why would someone select separate people for these guardianship roles? You might feel the person best suited to be intimately caring and bonding with your child every day is not the best money manager. In some cases, this division is handled by appointment of a guardian for the child with a financial trust set up that is handled by a trustee who pays support to the guardian and other bills for the child according to the trust terms and the trustee's discretion.

Single parents with sole custody who pass away have an even more important role in this process. Should you die, your child's other parent might have the legal right to the child, but there are exceptions. For example, if the child's other parent has never had an active role in the child's life, the other parent might not be named guardian if the court finds that it is not in the child's best interest.

Expectations for guardians

Before you select guardians for your children, take note of what their responsibilities will be. In short, they will need to do and provide for your children just as you would have as their parent.

The guardian is responsible for raising the child and looking after any of the child's assets.

At the time of your death, the guardian needs to petition the court for guardianship. The court might insist on a performance bond, which works much like the bond an executor has, to ensure the child will be well cared for. The guardian needs to take inventory of the child's assets, which would include any property received during the probate process or from a will, as well as any benefits from insurance policies, social security survivorship benefits, and retirement accounts.

The guardian then assumes the role of the parent in all aspects of the child's life. This includes managing all assets left to the child and ensuring the child's education, support, day-to-day care, and emotional care are provided for.

The guardian will continue in this role until it is no longer necessary; usually, this is when the child turns 18. While the child is still a minor, the guardian is responsible for reporting about the child's assets to courts as required and filing income tax claims as required by law on behalf of the child. The court will likely require that an annual report be submitted detailing the child's current assets and documenting any change in them. The funds from the child's assets can be used to pay for the care of the child including day-to-day costs and special purchases, such as buying the child his or her first vehicle or paying for educational expenses.

Trusts and Children

As has been mentioned, a trust is a legal tool that serves to hold and protect assets you leave behind. In this context, a trust is formed to help you protect your child's assets. A minor is not permitted to hold assets in his or her own right until he or she reaches the age of majority — in most states age 18. For this reason, the minor's assets are subject to management by a guardian. A trust makes it more difficult for a guardian to have a free hand with the money, an especially important safeguard with large amounts of money such as a large life insurance payout.

What will a trust do for your child? First, a trust will help to manage the assets including all funds, real estate, and other items you leave to your child or children when you die. It can also distribute the property to the child, or children, as you determine in your will when the child reaches 18 years of age, or an older age if you choose.

The trustee is responsible for accounting for the trust funds, filing tax returns, and keeping records of investments, disbursements, and income. The trustee you name can be an individual or an institution such as a bank. If you select an institution to manage the trust, they will do so professionally and will submit the required annual documents to your child's guardians. Most will also help with filing tax returns and other requirements.

How is a trust established?

A trust can be established by will (testamentary trust) or as a separate entity (inter vivos, or living trust). For example, suppose Dave and Laura wrote their will so if one of them passes away while they have minor children, the children are cared for. If Dave dies, all of his property goes first to Laura, then to the trust. If Laura dies, all of her property goes to Dave and then to the trust. So, if Dave dies and Laura dies, all of their property is reverted into a trust for their children. In this scenario, they have worked with their local bank, Main Street Bank, to set up the trust with the bank acting as the trustee. Their children, Michael and Suzy, are the beneficiaries of the trust. The trustee arranges for Michael and Suzy to receive financial allotments to provide for their care as necessary. These funds are provided to their guardian, David's brother.

Once Michael and Suzy get older, things change. When Michael, the older, reaches 22, he will receive half of what is then in the trust. Suzy will continue to receive allotments to her guardian for her care until she reaches 22, when the remaining trust property will be distributed to her.

There are various ways to set up such a trust to account for the disbursement of the funds. These decisions are made by you now and will be enforced by the will trustee. In addition to such requirements, special requests can also be made by you to provide for your children. For example, a payout can be put in place to allow your children's guardian to make home improvements to create space for your children. You can put in place a special payout yearly for family vacations and holiday costs. Trusts really have limitless possibilities when it comes to caring for your children, which is why so many people use them over simply handing over their assets to the child's guardian.

To create a trust, the trustor, or grantor, creates a legal document that places the described property into the trust for the benefit of the named beneficiary, in this case the minor child. A trustee is named to hold the property, take care of it, manage it, and disburse it, according to the terms of the trust.

The Uniform Transfers to Minors Act

The Uniform Transfers to Minors Act (UTMA) is another vehicle to use to transfer property to a minor. Under UTMA, a person is a minor until age 21 (25 in California). All forms of property can be transferred to a minor in the care of a custodian to be kept on the minor's behalf until he or she attains the age of majority. A gift under UTMA can be made during your lifetime or in your will. It is generally used for relatively small gifts that are easily managed. Large sums of money intended for investment or property that requires much care and maintenance are better suited for being held through a formal trust arrangement.

The Family Pot Trust

Another option for you to consider is the family pot trust. Here, all funds left from the estate are placed into one "pot" to be used by the trustee caring for your children. The ages of the children do not matter, as the trust is designed for care of both younger and older children. There is no rule that states the funds must be equally divided among the children.

So why would you want one child to potentially benefit more than another? Although it might seem disparate, the reality is that most families do not spend money equally among their children. Some children might need money spent for a medical procedure while another family might need to spend more money for a child who needs additional tutoring. Here, you leave discretion with the trustee, who is in charge of making decisions as he or she determines to be appropriate for each child's situation.

The pot trust is a desirable option if you have several younger children who are close in age. When the youngest child reaches the age of 18, the funds remaining in the trust are divided equally to each child. If the children are close in age, they should receive the funds from the remaining trust within a few years of turning 18. Keep in mind, if you do not want your children to receive funds at the age of 18, the family pot trust is not the right option for you. There is no way to extend the age limit here.

Summing Up

You have come to a point where you need to take stock and make decisions. How do you wish to have your children's lives managed if you die prematurely? Who will you appoint to care for them? How will you leave property to your children? By will, trust, or a combination of these measures? Discuss your thoughts about the options with legal counsel to determine which type of estate plan provides you the most comfort.

Chapter 9

Will Challenges

ven with advanced planning and the best attorney, wills can be contested or challenged by disgruntled heirs. Because your property is your own and you have the right to make your own will, it is essential to ensure your will is written in such a way as to avoid potential conflicts. The good news is the person contesting your will carries the burden of proof. This means that unless it fails to be properly drafted, such as if it lacks witnesses or your signature, your will is presumed valid until proved otherwise.

It is not easy to contest a will. If the will is determined to be invalid, the proceeds from the estate are left in the hands of the probate court to administer under intestate succession rules. Those who are heirs are most likely to receive most of the estate's property. Or, if there is an earlier version of your will, it could be put in place instead of the newer version.

Common Reasons Wills Are Contested

Competency

Mental competency is determined by several things, including the fact that you know you are making a will, you understand the value of your property, you know the people who are most likely to be included in the will, and you understand what it means to list these beneficiaries in your will.

Proving incompetency requires evidence, usually expert medical testimony, that the testator was not sufficiently mentally sound to create a will. Friends and family members might be asked to recall their observations. The witnesses to the will might need to testify as to their observations of the testator's words and conduct when they witnessed the will.

Although contesting a will has a bad connotation, in truth, it is often a good thing that such an opportunity exists. For example, an individual in the early stages of Alzheimer's disease might be competent enough to write a will. An individual in the later stages could be subjected to coercion or fraud by some unscrupulous person. To protect yourself from such claims, it is best for you to show proof of your mental stability at the time you wrote the will, especially if at any point in your life you have had health issues.

Coercion

Another reason why someone might contest your will is the belief that you were subjected to abuse or "undue influence" and therefore are not writing a will that reflects your free intent.

Undue influence is a term used to describe that someone has placed a lot of pressure on the testator to favor that person or the person's agenda. Undue influence is not easy to prove.

If the testator is experiencing physical or mental distress at the time he or she writes the will, the individual might be more likely to fall for the trickery of a dishonest person. If the testator is kept from other family members and friends, this too can make it easier for undue influence to occur.

Here is an example of how undue influence may happen insidiously. The testator consults an attorney to prepare the will. The attorney, who should be trustworthy, places clauses in the will that allow a member of the attorney's family to receive funds from your estate at the time of your death. Perhaps you did not read the final will closely or were unable to understand it due to illness. This is an example of an unethical lawyer and a case in which the court is likely to rule in favor of the contest of your will.

The most problematic of all undue influence cases are those that involve your children. If you decide to leave more property to one of your children than the others, it is often important to include an explanation for the disparity. This can be stated briefly in the will or by explanatory letter.

Consider this situation: A fun-loving widower with three adult children makes out his will. While he was alive, the children were good to him, but they were often too busy to visit. The man, looking for companionship, befriends a young man who becomes his "adopted son." This young man has no negative plans against the older man and is friendly. Because he lives nearby, he stops by often to help the older man with various tasks around the house. When the man dies, it is found that he has left behind a large estate. His children, showing their love at the funeral, though none of them had been to see their father in the last six months, were astonished to learn that their father had included the "adopted son" for an equal share of the estate in his will.

The children contested the will claiming the "adopted son" tried to force their father into including him in the will by undue influence. They were angry and felt disinherited by the share of the estate left to the outsider. The will was held valid, but the sons remained angry with their father and never understood why he would "slight" them in this way. As you can see, it is helpful to outline specific goals and sometimes to leave comments explaining them.

The will is poorly written, incomplete, or ambiguous

Another reason a will can be contested is poor drafting. Even with great care exerted, mistakes can happen. Some common mistakes in will preparation include:

- Not having proper witnesses

- Selecting the wrong witnesses (do not use witnesses who are gaining from your will's proceeds, for example)

- Having witnesses to sign your will but not at the same time or in your presence

- Not having two competent adult witnesses — the usual minimum requirement

With the witnesses in the room, you sign your will. Then, they sign your will in front of you. If this is not done, the will's validity might be contested.

Finally, if you fail to use a self-proving clause in the will, as provided in some states, this too can be grounds for contention. The witnesses sign a document that usually begins with "Under Penalties for Perjury" and then lists what the witnesses declare by signing your will. This includes that the will was signed by you, that both witnesses are present, and that you and they are free from any involuntary act forcing their hand. Some state statutes provide self-proving form language.

The witnesses have the task of ensuring the will was signed by you and you were in sound mind when signing it.

In addition to having reliable, appropriate witnesses, ensure your will is written properly. If you scratch anything out, the will can be invalidated. Therefore, keep the will in its original form, and if you want to add something to the document, amend the will by preparing a codicil or writing a new will. Remember, the codicil must be drafted and executed in the same manner as the original will, though it need not have the same witnesses.

If you believe there are grounds for your will to be contested on this level, have an attorney look it over and ensure your will is valid. You should have an attorney read through your will, even if you are writing it yourself, to ensure it is fully valid.

Potential Mistakes You Might Make

It is important to not let your feelings dominate your will. Writing hurtful things in your will can emotionally devastate people close to you. Before making any major decisions, consider the effect your choices will have on those you leave behind.

One good example of a mistake in a will is leaving abusive remarks about someone. You might truly hate someone and want to leave him or her out of your will, but being abusive in your will is uncalled for. More so, it could cause the individual additional harm because wills are public documents anyone can read after your death. For example, suppose a father is angered with whom his son chooses as a wife, and as a result, the father leaves some colorful language in his will and cuts the son out of all inheritance. Over the next few years, the father gets to know his daughter-in-law and his opinion of her changes. Then, he has a sudden heart attack and dies. The will was never changed, and now, when the will is read, the colorful and hateful feelings the father once felt toward his daughter-in-law are out in the open. She is hurt, and nothing can take back those remarks.

As mentioned in prior sections, there is no rule that says you have to leave something to everyone in your will. You can leave people out, including your children. But if you do so, make a note of this omission in your explanatory letter. By explaining your decision to disinherit this person, you avoid the threat of the will being contested.

If you make any arrangements with anyone over the next years of your life, such as promising something to him or her from your estate, be sure you have this included in your will. One of the most common mistakes an individual can make is not making note of these promises in the will. When the will maker dies, the person promised the property is angry and is likely to contest the will. Rather than leaving this open-ended, make a contract with the individual that can be followed by the executor of your will and make note of the contract in your will.

Making changes to the will

Changing your will is likely something you will have to do from time to time. Be sure you do so properly. As has been noted, you can only change your will in two ways: amend it with a codicil or make a new will. Codicils are handy for making singular changes, such as a new executor, or adding a specific bequest. If you are making several changes, a new will would be less confusing.

You should never make changes to your original document or a completed codicil, including scratching out words or changing the file.

CASE STUDY:
AN ATTORNEY'S ANECDOTE

Leland Ammons
Attorneys and Counselors at Law
Dallas, Texas
dfwlaw@dfwlaw.net

Leland Ammons, an attorney in Dallas, Texas, chuckles as he begins to tell a story from his probate experiences.

Ammons related a story about a wealthy Houston lady who hated her son-in-law. The woman in question had inherited her fortune and wanted to ensure her daughter would be provided for after she died. Additionally, the heiress wanted to make sure her daughter's husband would not be able to challenge her will on any grounds. The woman was concerned that the daughter's dominating husband would exert influence over any money she left to her daughter in the will, when she fully intended for the money to benefit only her daughter. In order to avoid this, the woman came up with an interesting plan.

The woman was convinced her son-in-law would challenge the will the minute she was in the ground, so every year she came to Ammons and had a new will drawn up at a cost of $2,500. The plan was if the son-in-law ever was successful at challenging her present will on competency grounds, the last previous will would become valid. As Ammons tells the story, by now, she has done 35 of the wills, which means they could have up to 35 trials to prove she was incompetent in each of 35 years, an unlikely result. Additionally, each time the woman makes a new will, she also writes a check to her son-in-law for $2,500 and sends it to him with a note thanking him for all the wonderful things he has done for her daughter. If he ever tries to declare her incompetent, he will be faced with testifying under oath that he cashed checks from an "incompetent woman."

In this case, the client has a level of fear and paranoia of a family member that prompts her to take countermeasures in advance to avoid a will contest. They are legal, and she can afford it to give herself some piece of mind with her plan.

No Contest Clauses

One drafting approach to dampen the ardor of would-be contestors to your will is to include a no-contest clause in the will. This provision states that anyone named in the will who challenges it shall lose any inheritance he or she might otherwise have received. Here is an example of such a clause from the last will and testament of actor Paul Newman:

"If any beneficiary under this will and/or any codicil hereto ("my will") and/or under my Trust Agreement, shall in any manner, directly or indirectly, attempt to contest the probate or validity of any part or all of my will and/or my Trust Agreement, then such beneficiary shall forfeit and cease to have any right or interest whatsoever under my will, and, in such event, I direct that my estate shall be disposed of in all respects as if such beneficiary had predeceased me."

Chapter 10

Special Considerations

lthough there are many good reasons to prepare one's will, certain special circumstances make the task even more compelling. To ensure your wishes will be carried out in these situations, your will needs to direct how they will be handled.

Dependents with Special Needs

Disabled children or adult disabled dependents such as a spouse require special consideration in your estate planning. The legal definition of a disabled person is one suffering from a severe and chronic physical situation or mental impairment and whose condition is likely to continue indefinitely. Each disabled individual has his or her own special needs. Some require the aid of a guardian; others are mentally fit to make their own decisions but are unable to support themselves financially or need physical assistance with daily living activities.

The planning you do for your disabled dependents depends on their needs and your means. There are so many unique circumstances that there is no way for this book to cover all possible circumstances. The provisions you make in your will and other estate planning instruments must be specific to your dependent's particular requirements coordinated with other forms of assistance that may be available as well.

One critical need is financial assistance for children. Many children face costly medical conditions. Even in a family that has quality health insurance, some conditions can be expensive, and the family often must turn to the government for assistance. This is beneficial as long as you are alive to provide necessary funds for your child's health requirements. If you die, you probably want your child to continue to receive these government benefits. For this reason, it often becomes necessary to ensure their needs are covered in your will or through a trust in such a way that government benefit eligibility continues.

If the child directly gains valuable property from your estate, chances are good that the child's net worth will increase, even if he or she has no substantial liquid assets. Still, because he or she has inherited these assets, the child might no longer qualify for the needed government financial benefits. Therefore, consider controlling the flow of inheritance through a trust arrangement.

If you include a disabled dependent as a beneficiary in your will, whether a minor or an adult, make provisions to ensure continuous care. One consideration is naming a guardian. It is important to speak frankly with the individual whom you wish to become the guardian because this is a large financial responsibility; it is also a commitment of personal time, attention and emotional support. It is not a responsibility for just anyone.

You also should make specific arrangements in terms of a disabled dependent's assets. Take some time to look over the beneficiaries you have listed in your will, on your retirement plans, your investment plans, life insurance policies, and for any other assets you have. If you intend to set aside specific assets for a disabled child and other assets for nondisabled beneficiaries, make sure you do not identify these gifts in generic terms. For example, a gift simply left to "my children" does not differentiate between the needs of the disabled child and other nondisabled children. If you intended it to be distributed more specifically, your intent is ambiguous and needs to be amended to specify how you want it divided.

It is not advisable to leave all of your assets to your nondisabled children and give them responsibility of caring for their disabled sibling. A financial consideration that counsels against this is that your nondisabled children could have debts of their own that need to be settled. Money and other assets you allocate to them to care for a sibling with special needs become part of their own estates. Therefore, what were originally your assets would be susceptible to the nondisabled children's creditors and possibly subject to attachment in divorce proceedings. A more personal consideration is that leaving it up to the disabled child's siblings is uncertain, no matter how much you trust them or how genuine their commitment. Their own circumstances can change, including early death, that leave the disabled child without provision.

A better approach is to create a trust for your disabled child during your lifetime (a living trust) or in your will (a testamentary trust). Under this arrangement, if you die, the property is still available to your disabled child to use and is sheltered from others' creditors. Siblings can be named as trustees if you wish. The trust can provide that in the event of the disabled child's death, the trust property will pass on to those you list as beneficiaries. This allows the home and/or other assets placed in trust to be used by your disabled child during his or her lifetime.

Although you are gone, you have maintained control over both the care of the disabled child and the property.

In making these plans, it is advisable to consult carefully with counsel and estate planners to ensure the best arrangement for the child is crafted to maximize benefits available from all sources.

Same-sex Unions

The laws on same-sex marriages and civil unions are changing. Therefore, it is essential to consider how the laws in your state define the rights of an individual living with you as a life partner. You cannot inherit from each other as spouses unless you are in a jurisdiction that recognizes same-sex marriage with spousal rights afforded to the partners. A few states recognize same-sex unions. Massachusetts recognizes same-sex marriage, and Vermont recognizes same-sex civil unions.

Unless state law expressly affords spousal rights of inheritance to same-sex partners who have formalized their union, the couple has no legal claim on each other's assets when one dies. Other mechanisms, such as joint ownership with survivorship rights can be used for specific property and bank accounts, but unless there is provision for a partner in a will, the partner will have no death benefit rights under the law.

Committed couples should provide for each other in their wills. This is all the more compelling a necessity for these relationships. Otherwise, more than loss of a partner will occur when one dies. For example, suppose Joan and Elizabeth live together as a monogamous couple for 20 years. They share their household, their possessions, and their lives together.

Joan never gets around to making her will. When they joined as a couple, Joan already owned their condo. Elizabeth has shared the cost, maintenance fees, and expenses of the condo during their 20 years together. They never got around to putting the condo in a joint survivorship deed arrangement. Joan dies first. Their state does not recognize same sex marriage or even civil unions. All of Joan's possessions including the condo pass by intestate succession to her disapproving siblings who have not spoken to either Joan or Elizabeth for the entire 20 years of their relationship. As a result, Elizabeth loses her home as well as her partner. She can try to make an equitable claim for her contribution to the financial upkeep of the condo, but it is likely her investment would be viewed simply as her payment of "rent" as a roommate. The law does not account for this situation in terms of rights of inheritance. In this scenario, Joan's surviving next of kin are her siblings. Had the couple engaged in even rudimentary estate planning, this result would have been far different.

At a minimum, both partners need to make provision for each other in their wills. If the relationship should end before either of them dies, as many relationships do regardless of gender, they can update their wills and provide for alternative beneficiaries.

If you are concerned about a family member challenging your will, make sure you address any questions you have with your attorney. It might be beneficial to you and your partner to create a living trust and use joint and survivorship ownership mechanisms as well as life insurance. These nonprobate vehicles will not be subject to challenge in a probate proceeding.

Common Law Marriage

The same limitations of same-sex couples apply to individuals of opposite sex who are living together unless they live in one of the few states that recognizes common law marriage and all the rules evidencing a common law marriage are satisfied for their state.

The following states recognize common law marriage:

- Alabama
- Colorado
- Georgia (marriages established before January 1, 1997)
- Idaho (marriages established before January 1, 1996)
- Iowa
- Kansas
- Montana
- New Hampshire (recognized only for inheritance rights)
- Ohio (marriages established before October 10, 1991)
- Oklahoma (marriages established before October 1, 1998, but court decisions indicate later marriages might be recognized)
- Pennsylvania (marriages established before January 1, 2001)
- Rhode Island
- South Carolina
- Texas
- Utah
- Washington, D.C.

Each state defines its own specific requirements that must be satisfied to constitute common law marriage. Common elements are the partners holding themselves out publicly as husband and wife and cohabitation. Merely living together for a period of time while making it clear that you are not married will not satisfy any test. There must be intent to be married, actual cohabitation, and living together as married with a reasonable public perception of a marriage. If you live in one of the above states and have a relationship that you believe qualifies as common law marriage, consult an attorney to determine if your situation indeed meets the common law marriage requirements for your state.

If a couple's situation satisfies the common law marriage requirements, their status becomes the same as a formal marriage. All marital rights attach, including inheritance, unless the state has limited these rights in some way.

Sudden Riches or Debt

Suppose you win the lottery or your rich Uncle Ben leaves you a large inheritance. Such good fortune would affect your estate planning, including tax planning. Tax consequences alone could ultimately deplete your estate far more than necessary.

Conversely, reversal of fortune has its effect. Assume you filed for bankruptcy today. Your debts are wiped out, and you are free and clear, but you have also lost most of your assets. Bequests in your current will at this point are moot. Now, over time, you will again begin to build your worth and your assets. Your will should be updated to reflect these changes.

If you file for bankruptcy, note that life insurance and most retirement plans will not be liquidated for bankruptcy claims. In other words, you still need to have beneficiaries listed on these accounts to receive the payout at the time of your death. Those funds are not lost in the bankruptcy process. In addition, most states do allow you to keep some assets. The amount of assets you are allowed to keep differs from state to state. Anything you are able to keep, such as a home and car, personal property, or other assets, can be provided for in your will.

Divorce

Suppose a married couple has wills in place leaving all or a substantial portion of their estates to each other. What happens if they divorce and one or both of them forget to update their wills?

In most states, divorce automatically revokes a will provision bequeathing property to the former spouse divorced after the date of the will. Generally, the entire will is not revoked, but the law of your state should be checked to confirm this point.

The best approach is not to rely on this statutory revocation of will provisions benefitting a divorced spouse. The better approach is to update the will as soon as possible following the final court decree of divorce. In some cases, a person might wish to still include a former spouse as a beneficiary in his or her will. The new will is even more important in this event, to overcome the automatic statutory revocation by divorce.

Debts and Taxes

Everyone hates taxes, and no one likes being in debt, but both are part of every estate. Therefore, they should be considered when writing your will. Part of writing your will should include giving your executor instructions on how to handle the debts you leave behind. Estimate what your debts are likely to be at the time of your death. For substantial debt or special personal liabilities, it is wise to provide guidance to your executor. Some of your assets can be protected from unsecured debt, depending on the state of jurisdiction.

In addition to accounting for debts and taxes, estate planning must recognize the cost of dying, including funeral costs, burial, and other arrangements. The costs of these expenses range widely, but a certainty is that they continue to rise. In addition, there will be probate and administration fees, even with a will. These costs can and should be foreseen in estate planning. Your will can designate how they should be paid, and you can choose the assets to be used, if necessary, to cover these costs.

How debts are paid after death

When an estate is filed for probate, with or without a will, one of the tasks of the executor or court appointed administrator is publishing notice of the estate to creditors. The methods of notification and time periods vary slightly by state, but generally, the notice is required early in the estate process. The creditors then have a limited time, ranging from three to nine months depending on the jurisdiction, to make their claims for payment to the estate. The executor's job is to then verify the claims, settle upon an agreed amount with each creditor, and pay off the debts. When the period for this process expires, no more claims can be made against the estate.

Debts usually have a certain priority as well. The funeral expenses, taxes, court costs, appraisal fees (if any), executor fees (if any), and attorney fees generally stand ahead of creditors. Secured debts stand ahead of general unsecured debts.

As you make out your will, keep in mind how debts are likely to factor into it. There are two specific types of debts that need to be considered: secured and unsecured debts.

Unsecured debt

Unsecured debt is the most common form of debt and is not tied to any asset. This includes credit cards, utilities, and medical bills. The executor pays each of these debts out of your probate estate.

Secured debt

Secured debts are indemnified by specific property. The debt must be paid before the property can belong to the owner free and clear because the lender has a security interest in the property until the debt is paid. The most common type of secured debt for individuals is real estate mortgage. Other types include vehicles, larger appliances or electronics, business equipment, and business loans for which you are an indemnifier, co-signer, or the primary debtor.

To avoid foreclosure on secured debts, provide specific directions in your will that state how they should be paid. One method is to specify life insurance proceeds to cover a mortgage.

Listing several resources for debt payment

As you consider which resources will pay for each of your debts, keep in mind the value of those resources and the amount of debt you must pay off. The order in which the debts are paid is often important to specifically outline. For example, if you have savings accounts, stocks, and bonds, and you leave behind debt, which of these assets will be used to pay debts? You can designate how you would like your debts paid by listing the order of assets to be used to satisfy them. In this way, you simplify the process for your executor and preserve certain assets you want intact.

Estate and inheritance taxes

Unless a statutory exemption or exclusion applies, an estate will be subject to federal and/or state estate tax liability. The year 2010 was unique because it had no federal estate tax in place until December 17, 2010 when Congress reinstated an estate tax scheme retroactive to January 1, 2010 and prospective through 2010. Estates up to $5 million are exempt. Then they are taxed at 35 percent.

Additionally, most states have an estate tax as well, though several are in tax limbo at the time of publication because they are tied to the federal tax scheme, which has just changed.

Estate taxes are paid out of the estate. A few states have what is called inheritance tax. This is a tax levied on the beneficiaries to pay based on the amount of inheritance they receive. This is typically set by state statute on a sliding scale, with close relatives paying less tax than more remotely related persons.

The following chart illustrates the states that have inheritance taxes and how they are imposed.

State	Are spouses exempt?	Are descendants exempt?	Are domestic partners exempt?	Is life insurance included?	Tax rate	Tax form	Due date
Indiana	Yes	No	No	No	1% to 20%	Form IH-6	9 months after death
Iowa	Yes	Yes	No	No	5% to 15%	Form IA 706	9 months after death
Kentucky	Yes	Yes	No	No	4% to 16%	Form 92A200, 92A202, or 92A205	18 months after death
Maryland	Yes	Yes	Certain transfers	No	10%	Varies	Varies

State	Are spouses exempt?	Are descendants exempt?	Are domestic partners exempt?	Is life insurance included?	Tax rate	Tax form	Due date
Nebraska	Yes	No	No	No	1% to 18%	Form 500	12 months after death
New Jersey	Yes	Yes	Yes	No	11% to 16%	Form IT-R or IT-NR	8 months after death
Pennsylvania	Yes	No	No	No	4.5% to 15%	Form REV-1500	9 months after death

In the News: Estate Taxes

There was also no federal estate tax in 2010 until December 17, 2010, when Congress passed the Tax Relief, Unemployment Insurance Reauthorization, and Job Creation Act of 2010, which was signed into law by President Obama. This bill reinstated the federal estate tax for estates valued at over $5 million, retroactive to January 1, 2010. Congress' action was a last-minute measure to avoid the government's estimated loss of billions in tax revenue.

The law gives executors of 2010 estates a choice of tax rules to apply: (1) the Act's reinstated tax scheme, which exempts estates up to $5 million and imposes a tax on those exceeding the exemption at 35 percent; or (2) the 2010 estate can opt out of estate taxes and instead take a modified carry-over tax basis value of property inherited by beneficiaries of the estate.

The second option means valuing inherited property for the beneficiary's income tax purposes at less than its fair market value at time of inheritance. Under the usual rule, when a beneficiary inherits property, the beneficiary takes the property at its "stepped up" tax basis, i.e., the property value at the time of inheritance. Thus, there is no capital gain accrued to the beneficiary for the property's increase in value from the time the decedent acquired it. Under the 2010 modified carry-over option, the valuation is the lesser of the fair market value of the property on the date of date (the stepped-up value) or the decedent's original tax basis of the property plus the value of improvements made to the property. For example, John bought a piece of land for $1,000,000 20 years before he died.

John makes no improvements to the property; he just holds on to it. At time of John's death, when his son inherits it, the property is worth $2,000,000 fair market value. Normally his son would take the property at the "stepped up" $2,000,000 value. Under the new law's modified carry-over option for 2010 estates, the "lesser value" is $1,000,000. John's son has a gain of $1 million under this option.

This choice becomes relevant for estates exceeding $5,000,000, such as the late George Steinbrenner's $1.5 billion estate. Steinbrenner's death in 2010 could save his estate (and thus his heirs) millions in taxes under option No. 2. Whether the heirs fare better under option No. 2 will depend on the property holdings of the estate and how they are passed on to heirs for tax purposes. The executor will have to calculate which option works to best financial advantage.

For estates in 2011 and 2012, as the law stands now, the federal estate and gift tax exemptions are combined at $5 million per individual, with the tax rate set at 35 percent. However, the Act's provisions are temporary and Congress will have to reconsider the estate tax scheme yet again in 2012.

As you plan your will, the point to remember is that there could well be a tax implication affecting the ultimate net value of your estate. Because these laws change frequently, you must consult legal counsel to find out how taxes will affect your estate and will planning, if at all. Find out if your estate is likely to be subject to a federal estate tax or whether that is even possible to project. Find out what your state has in place for estate taxes and inheritance taxes. Many people find themselves needing to update their wills and estate trust plans just to keep up with changes in the tax laws.

Estate taxes are paid in the same way you pay your debts. You can allow your executor to pay your taxes for you, which is usually what happens because the taxes on estates are usually low. If you would like to be in more control through your will, you can leave a step-by-step payment option for your taxes. This is the same process you use to pay your debts.

One of the benefits of having your executor handle your taxes on your behalf is that the executor is able to make decisions based on the current circumstances that might have changed since the last time you updated your will. The executor does have the ability to sell property or cash in assets to pay your taxes in this case. If you wish to make sure specific gifts are not sold and make it to your listed beneficiaries, you can state in your will that certain gifts are unable to be used for taxes. This may not be enforceable if taxes exceed the value of assets you set aside in the estate to pay them.

CASE STUDY: WRITING YOUR WILL

Elaine Richards
Boston, Massachusetts

Elaine Richards created her will in 2006 after she was diagnosed with diabetes. "I have no family and wanted to make an arrangement for disposing of my personal property," she said. Because Richards works at a law firm, she also did not need to hire an attorney, accountant, or any of the other professionals many people use to put a will and estate plan together.

"We had examples of wills in our computer, so I rewrote one to suit my needs," she added. "I also wanted to write my will in a special way so my personal possessions would be sold and the money given to my beneficiary," she said. "As a single person, I wanted a friend who knew my wishes to have a health care proxy as well." A health care proxy is a document that gives a person you trust the ability to make decisions regarding your health care if you become unable to make such decisions.

Richards' personal property did not include real estate. Richards said her assets consisted of a savings account and many antiques. "I'm a single person with only one salary," she explained. "I don't have 'assets' except my antiques and collectibles. I wanted to name someone who knows the Internet and could sell my goods and keep the money from such a sale. I wanted to leave the person a 'salary' for sell-ing my goods and money to pay my rent for six months while this was being done. This serves the purpose of getting my goods removed from my apartment and leaving the proceeds to a friend, as I have no local family to perform this function."

Richards said she believes it is important to leave a record of one's wishes even if he or she does not have a large estate. One of the rea-sons she chose a friend to handle her estate when she dies is she lives in a different state than many of her friends and her distant family.

"I have no one to empty my apartment when I am gone, so it is important that I make special provisions for that," she added. Also, Richards has no children, either underage or grown; this was another consideration that spurred her to consider a good friend in the Boston area to clean out her apartment and sell the items that she owns. Her main concern was providing that person an incentive for doing it.

"I needed someone local, whom I trusted, and whom I wanted to have the income from the sale of my goods," she said. She chose only one person because, as she said, "I have known too many families who have had disagreements when several people are involved."

Make Note of Your Circumstances

In planning for your will and estate, make note of any special circumstances in your life that you want to address. These may require special planning and examination of options.

Are you unsure of how to plan for something? Nearly all goals can be met. Work with your attorney to meet them.

Putting it All Together

When you have worked through all the aspects of preparing information relevant for your will, you should have identified your assets, legal heirs, beneficiaries you want to designate in your will, and heirs you wish to disinherit. You should also have accounted for costs, such as legal fees, taxes, probate costs, funeral costs, and debts. At this point, you can now start putting the will together.

What type of will suits your needs? As reviewed in Chapter 2, there is more than one format. A fill-in-the-blank variety is appealing for its apparent simplicity. This one also lacks flexibility, though, and does not lend itself to specialized details. The best option is a customized will, which allows the testator originality of expression and control over the manner and conditions of distribution his or her possessions. Some clauses will be standard, consisting of legal "boilerplate," but the substantive areas of the will are unique to the testator's specific facts, family, and feelings.

Customization works well for those individuals who have specific ideas about the ways in which their properties should be distributed. You can still compile this will yourself, though using the skills and advice of an attorney is advisable. If you wish to accomplish any of the following things in your will, choose a customized will instead of a basic fill-in-the-blank style:

- You wish to establish two or more people to be executors in your will. Keep in mind this is not related to having an alternative backup executor. This means you wish for two or more people share the job as main executors and serve together at the time of your death, such as the executor appointment provision in President Kennedy's will.

- You wish to have more than two residuary beneficiaries between whom you are dividing the residue of the estate.

- You wish to forgive any debts in your will. This includes wishing to state why you are forgiving these debts in your will.

- You wish for your executor to post a bond to protect your beneficiary's property.

- You wish to name different people to serve as guardians for your child — for example, a guardian of property and guardian of person.

- You wish to leave behind evidence and explanation as to why a child's remaining parent is unfit to care for the child and that it is not in the child's best interest for this parent to be named the child's guardian.

- You wish to leave explanatory letters with the will.

- You wish to specifically outline how debts and taxes will be paid in your will. This includes leaving a specific order in which they should be paid.

- You wish to disinherit one or more of your children or anyone else who has an expectation of inheritance from you by law or by association with you in some manner.

- You wish to name your same-sex partner as your beneficiary.

- You wish to direct how the executor should handle an ademption.

- You wish to set up a testamentary trust.

- You wish to direct assets into a pour-over trust. *These will be discussed in Chapter 11.*

- You wish to bequeath a substantial portion of your estate to charity.

- You wish to direct which assets can be sold to cover debts and taxes.

- You wish to designate the attorney who will handle the estate with the executor.

- You wish to include a no-contest clause.

- You wish to provide for care for your pet or pets.

- You wish to do anything else considered unique or out of the norm.

- You have left frozen embryos, sperm, or ova behind for posthumous childbearing.

If you have other requirements for your will or you are hoping to do something different than what is listed here, work with your attorney to establish the best format. Some things are not legally allowable. Most wishes can be put into practice if included in the will properly.

Chapter 11

Using Trusts with Wills to Protect Assets

The will is a good investment of your time because it gives specific directions as to what should be done when you die and covers any loopholes in your estate plan. However, it is often not enough for a large estate or for special needs. In these situations, you need more financial control. A trust is a financial tool. A trust has the ability to ensure your estate directives are carried out now and that all of your assets are passed to your beneficiaries just as you would like them to be. A trust can help save money both through the method of funding the trust and by decreasing tax exposure.

A trust is a legal instrument that is able to hold and manage real property, tangible property, and intangible property. When property is transferred into the trust, the trust gains ownership of the property as a distinct entity. It holds the property for the benefit of the person(s) named as its beneficiary.

A trust can be created while you are alive (called an inter vivos or living trust), or you can set up a testamentary trust to be activated when you die, as you would a will. There are several benefits a trust offers that a will does not:

- Property can be managed through a living trust during your lifetime, while a will becomes effective at the time of your death.

- It can help to reduce the taxes the estate will have to pay if properly done.

- A trust allows you to avoid or minimize probate.

- It also allows for the simplified transfer of your assets to your beneficiaries at the time of your death or even during your lifetime, as you choose.

- A trust allows for more options in how you are able to move property to your beneficiaries. For example, through a trust, you can leave property to your children from a first marriage while ensuring a second spouse cannot lay claim to that property.

- Finally, a trust gives you more privacy. Wills are public records and are easily found by anyone interested in them. A trust is a private document unless it is part of the will.

A trust option is something to consider in conjunction with planning your will as part of your estate planning process.

A trust is useful for providing for minor children and disabled dependents. A trust is also a mechanism to preserve property within a family. A trust can also be a mechanism to manage your funds during your retirement years. Many people who wish to provide for themselves during their later years establish a trust to ensure there are resources available for them with a trustee to administer those resources. Every trust will have a trustee to administer the trust. Setting aside funds and appointing a trustee covers a situation where one can no longer provide for one's self.

The creator of the trust — called the settlor, trustor, or grantor — is the person who establishes the trust by funding it with money and/or other assets. The beneficiary of a trust is the person designated by the grantor to receive payouts of the principal and/ or interest of the property from the trust according to terms and conditions set forth by the grantor. The grantor names a trustee to hold the property, manage the trust, and distribute the property to the beneficiary according to the trust's requirements.

If you set up a trust for a named beneficiary, the trustee can be anyone you name, including a family member or a friend. It can also be your bank or your attorney. You should also name a successor trustee. This person is sometimes legally referred to as a surviving trustee. The successor trustee is a person who will assume the duties of the trustee should he or she die, become incapacitated, or otherwise become unable or unwilling to serve as trustee.

Testamentary Trust

A testamentary trust is created within the will, so it does not become effective or "alive" until your death. The assets you have decided to include in your trust are transferred to the trustee. This process is similar to what happens when you leave items in your will to beneficiaries.

In this form of a trust, the trust continues apart and beyond the probate process and holds its property for the trust's term. After the probate process, a standard will is closed up after the directives have been completed. As you can see, the benefit here is the fact that the trust goes on, serving your purpose for as long as the trust exists.

An example of a testamentary trust is one created in Walt Disney's will. The basic elements of the trust were stated using a portion of the residue of the estate, as follows:

"Forty-five percent (45%) of such residue shall be distributed to LILLIAN B. DISNEY, HERBERT F. STURDY and UNITED CALIFORNIA BANK as Trustees, IN TRUST. Such Trust shall be known as the Disney Family Trust and shall be held and distributed as provided for in Article SIXTH below."

This clause states the amount of the property that goes into the trust, names the trustees, and refers to the provisions of the trust (Article SIXTH) for the terms and beneficiaries. The Sixth Article of the will then sets forth all of the directions and limitations of the trust. To summarize, if his wife Lillian survives him, she is the primary beneficiary, followed by his daughters and grandchildren.

Another type of testamentary trust is one created to receive life insurance proceeds. The estate is named as beneficiary of the proceeds, and with the will's direction, they are paid into the testamentary trust. Such an arrangement must be made only with assistance of counsel; otherwise, there is a risk the trust will fail through some technical deficiency in how it is written up. Conversely, you can set up a living trust and bequeath assets in the will to the trust. The assets are said to "pour over" into the trust from the estate. Pour-over trusts can be created with minimal funding for purposes of being set up and then become active once the substantial funding pours in from the estate.

A detraction of the testamentary trust is the property goes through probate, where it is subject to creditors and expenses before the trust can be established.

The Living Trust

A living, or *inter vivos*, trust is created during your lifetime and can work as a partial substitute for a will. When you die, the trust survives to be distributed to its designated beneficiaries. Many people wish to establish the living trust to help provide for their children with a bit more control. A child who spends money too freely, one that is unable to manage money, or one who has an abuse problem can be the beneficiary of a trust that controls the flow and use of income. This is called a spendthrift trust. Situations such as these cannot be controlled easily through will conditions, but they can by trust terms.

The revocable living trust

One type of living trust is the revocable living trust. As the name indicates, this design gives you the ability to change your mind and dissolve or change the trust after creating it. With this form of trust, you can move property into and out of the trust freely. You can sell it, or you can spend it. These are your assets to use as you determine. With this form of trust, you can also change any of the terms of the trust.

The revocable living trust has several key benefits, one of which is the ability to avoid probate. This is because all of your assets will pass to your trust beneficiaries outside of probate at the time of your death. Secondly, as the creator of the trust, you can also serve as the trustee or name someone else as trustee at your discretion. This is an advantage because you retain control over the trust property.

Another benefit of the revocable living trust is the alternative trustee is able to serve when the trustee (or creator) is no longer able to do so. The trust is also able to receive assets from the creator, and it can receive assets from the creator's estate.

On the negative side, the revocable living trust does not give you a tax advantage. All of the income is taxed to the creator of the trust because it remains in his or her control. All assets of the trust are subject to estate taxes at the time of the creator's death. For those looking for a trust arrangement that helps them with tax avoidance, the revocable living trust is not the answer.

The irrevocable living trust

The irrevocable living trust, just as its name sounds, has some specific limitations. In this form of trust, the creator is able to make a gift of property while he or she is still alive. The gift is subject to federal gift tax paid by the donor. However, it is exempt from federal estate taxes. The biggest downside to this type of gift is that once the gift is given, it no longer is under the control of the trust's creator. Once an irrevocable living trust is put into place, there is no way to reverse it.

The irrevocable trust works well for those who have a large estate and want to minimize estate taxes as well as put the property into a specific controlled arrangement. If you can afford to give away those assets you own, using an irrevocable living trust is perhaps the most affordable option. Many use this to benefit their children and grandchildren.

The Bypass Trust

A bypass trust is a unique type of trust that can assist in decreasing tax obligations. It has been a favored vehicle in estate planning for this reason. The goal of this trust is to lessen or even eliminate the amount of estate taxes. One of the most popular forms of a bypass trust is the AB trust, used by married people who have a combined estate that exceeds the estate tax exemption threshold. These individuals would likely pay a significant amount of money in estate taxes if their properties were not somehow sheltered.

The bypass trust is established the same way any other trust is established. It becomes effective at death. Your spouse is generally named as the beneficiary of your trust, though it does not have to be your spouse. This person, called the life beneficiary, has some rights to the property within the trust throughout his or her life. Any property added to the estate is part of your taxable property. In most cases, there are no taxes assessed on your property at the time of your death, regardless of what year it is. The life beneficiary never legally owns the property in the trust, and this is where the bypass trust can become incredibly important. Because of this benefit, when the life beneficiary dies, the property is not legally part of their estate, even though they might have used it throughout that time. Therefore, there are no estate taxes levied on the property when the life beneficiary dies.

If the same property passed through probate under your will, taxes would have been assessed at that time. Then, when your spouse dies, the property now in his or her rightful ownership would be transferred in turn to his or her beneficiaries and subject to estate tax. This subjects the same assets to estate taxes twice before they would reach their final beneficiaries.

The individual named as a life beneficiary is generally a spouse. That person is given the amount of rights to the property as described in the document. There are many ways you can use this. For example, the life beneficiary might have the rights to all of the income from the trust. Or, the beneficiary might only be allowed to use the property or might be limited by how much he or she can spend. You can also specify the amount of trust income to be used to pay for the life beneficiary's medical expenses or end-of-life care.

In many situations, the trust's life beneficiary and the trustee are the same person. However, they can be two different people. In this case, the trustee still directs how the funds within the trust will be used.

Keep in mind that the life beneficiary is given the rights to use the property however the creator of the trust determines. Because that individual never owns the property, he or she cannot pass it by will to someone else or use it outside the limitations of the trust. The beneficiary has no power to change the terms of the trust.

For example, suppose Lynn and Fred are married. Lynn creates a bypass trust. She puts half of her assets in trust with Fred as the life beneficiary and their son Tim as the remainder beneficiary. When Lynn dies, Fred will be able to use any and all of Lynn's property. For example, he is able to live in their home, he can collect income from her investments to use as needed, and he can use the property to pay for his medical expenses. When Fred dies, Lynn's property does not go through his estate because Fred did not own it outright. Rather, at that time, the trust's decree is that the property is passed to Tim as the final beneficiary.

Consider what would have happened if Lynn had not used this bypass trust. Her estate, valued at $2.5 million, would have been willed to Fred at her death. As a result, Fred's estate value would have increased to $4 million when both his and her estates were added together because his estate was worth $1.5 million. Then, when Fred died, the value of the combined estates would be much higher and subject to estate taxes based on $4 million, rather than $1.5 million.

Limitations of bypass trusts

The Internal Revenue Service has rules limiting bypass trusts. For example, the trustee does not possess complete discretion as to how the principal of the trust is spent. If the grantor wishes to give the trustee this type of financial freedom, the life beneficiary is treated as the owner of the property, which defeats the tax benefit. Even if the trust specifically states the trust's principal can be used for the well-being and comfort of the life beneficiary, the IRS will consider this an unascertainable standard and, therefore, will consider the beneficiary the owner of the property. At the time of the life beneficiary's death, the property is then levied by taxes. On the other hand, there are permitted stipulations. For example, the trustee is able to spend for the life beneficiary if the spending comes in the form of maintaining the health, education, support, or maintenance of the life beneficiary.

Most people who use a bypass trust have two goals. They want to ensure their spouse has the ability to maintain their standard of living and have the funds they need to meet their needs. At the same time, these individuals want to save as much of their estate from taxes as possible so it can be passed down to their final beneficiaries as in tact as possible. The only way to accomplish this is to use the proper terminology that satisfies the IRS's requirements. This is a workable limitation. For example, using the terms "support, health, and maintenance" gives the life beneficiary the ability to use the funds for just about any of his or her needs while meeting the IRS's requirements. As with any matter pertaining to taxes, though, keep abreast of current laws and regulations through consultation with your legal counsel. Regulations change.

5 and 5 power of the bypass trust

You might have heard talk about the "5 and 5 power" of the bypass trust. This term refers to the bypass trust trustee's ability to "invade" the trust just one time per year to obtain funds to use in any way. This is done on behalf of one or more of the beneficiaries. The 5 and 5 power gives the trustee the ability to remove up to 5 percent of the value of the principal or $5,000, whichever is greater. These funds can be used or removed by the trustee and given to the life beneficiary or the remainder beneficiaries.

It is imperative that the bypass trust specifically list who may benefit from the 5 and 5 power. When you work with your estate planning attorney, you might be advised against use of the 5 and 5 option because it gives the receiving beneficiary unlimited use of those funds once distributed. If your object is to conserve funds, reducing the trust 5 percent or $5,000 annually is counterproductive. Conservative estate planners view this as too much consistent depletion.

On the flip side, there is a clear benefit to the final beneficiaries you select because they have the ability to benefit from the trust prior to the death of the life beneficiary. If you think your remainder beneficiary might need the funds prior to the death of the life beneficiary, it might be a good thing to add the 5 and 5 provision into the trust. Moreover, there is no requirement that these funds be used in this way. No funds "have" to be removed using the 5 and 5 power.

AB Trusts

The AB trust is a type of trust for married couples that allows individuals to pass property to the surviving spouse while avoiding hefty tax consequences. With the AB trust, the surviving spouse is still able to benefit from the property and can use it as they would like for the rest of their lives. Yet, throughout this time, the surviving spouse is not the legal owner of the property and, therefore, will not have a heavy tax levied on the property after the second spouse dies. In short, the AB trust is similar to the bypass trust, but it is designed specifically for married couples. It is sometimes called a credit shelter trust or a marital life trust.

The use of an AB trust might be right for you if you have a valuable combined estate that you fear will be heavily taxed at the time of your death. To avoid this cost, each spouse will create an AB trust. In the will, each spouse leaves all of his or her property to the trust. They do not give it to the surviving spouse, as this would create ownership of the property. Rather, all — or the bulk — of the property is left to "Trust A."

When one spouse dies, the other gets only what is called the "life estate" interest in the estate left behind in Trust A. The surviving spouse keeps the revocable living trust, called "Trust B," intact.

In this situation, both spouses are able to list their beneficiaries (generally their children) for property they rightfully can leave behind. The ultimate beneficiaries will receive the property when the surviving spouse dies.

For example, suppose Ellen and Albert are married. They have an estate valued at $3 million. The personal exemption is set at $2 million when they die (this is just hypothetical because the exemption is a moving target). When Albert dies, their AB trust will go into effect. Both have left all of their property to each other, and their beneficiaries are their children (after they both die). When Albert dies, he has an estate valued at half of the total estate, or $1.5 million. Because he is passing this to his wife at death through the trust and it is under the personal exemption amount, there are no taxes levied on Albert's estate.

When Ellen dies, the estate is valued at $3 million (both estates combined), but Ellen's only ownership is in her $1.5 million. The other half is not owned by her, but by the trust. Because of the $2 million exemption, Ellen's estate does not have to pay any estate taxes. Therefore, the beneficiaries will receive the full $3 million, and taxes have been completely avoided.

This is an excellent benefit for those who wish to avoid the cost of estate tax at the time of death. The following are factors to consider when thinking about an AB trust:

- If your estate is worth more than the exemption, and you and your spouse both plan to leave the estate to each other, this is an ideal situation in which to establish the AB trust. Be sure to keep up to date on the personal exemption changes because this will affect who should use an AB trust.

- The AB trust is not a good option for those who plan to leave all of their property to their children or other beneficiaries and wish to restrict the use of the property by the surviving spouse. It will not accomplish this goal because the surviving spouse remains free to use the first spouse's property.

- Age can play a factor. There is little benefit in creating a trust when both of you or just one of the spouses is younger than 45 because the surviving spouse is likely to live for some time, and tying up property in a trust can make it more difficult to manage and might place limitations on this individual.

- There is a complex method of record-keeping required for an AB trust. If you do not wish for the individual to have to manage this paperwork, this type of trust might not be right for you.

- The entire family, including spouses and beneficiaries, needs to be aware of what is happening. The goal of the AB trust is to save on estate taxes, and it is therefore important to ensure everyone understands this and their role in the process. The surviving spouse has free ability to use the estate left to him or her. If this will cause strife in the family, you might want to reconsider whether this is a good fit for everyone involved.

As you can see, the AB trust might not be the right fit for everyone, but it is a great choice for those who can meet these requirements and need to conserve on estate taxes. Although it is best to work with an estate attorney familiar with the design of this trust, you can start to put together the trust on your own in order to have a working draft to discuss with legal counsel.

Creating an AB trust

To create an AB trust, both spouses need to agree to leave the estate to the other spouse. This type of trust can be designed within a living trust or alongside it. This helps the process go smoothly, and it also helps the estate avoid probate. Once the trust avoids probate, the irrevocable Trust A is put into place.

Within Trust A, each spouse needs to list property considered legally his or her own. In addition, half of any community-owned or co-owned property is divided. You can place any type of property in a trust like this. You can also leave any individual retirement accounts; though, with a 401(k), you will need to have a signed waiver from your spouse allowing the funds to pass to ownership of the trust, rather than to the spouse.

Once the first spouse dies, the property in the deceased spouse's Trust A is transferred to the AB trust, and the surviving spouse is charged with managing it. This trust becomes irrevocable. The surviving spouse must abide by all requirements and terms of the trust. The surviving spouse's Trust B remains revocable. This spouse can amend the living trust as long as he or she needs to or feels he or she should. Beneficiaries can be changed on the surviving spouse's trust. At the time of the death of the second spouse, all property within that individual's Trust B is sent to its final beneficiaries. All property in the first deceased spouse's Trust A is sent to its final beneficiaries.

When the trusts are created, it is common for the named trustee to be the other spouse, so the surviving spouse remains in full control of the other spouse's property after his or her death. Each spouse must be listed as the trustee on the other spouse's trust. In addition, there is often a successor trustee named. The successor would take control of the trusts should the surviving spouse become incapacitated. You can name someone other than your spouse as the trustee. This person will manage the property in the trust after the first spouse dies.

Bypass Trusts for Unmarried Individuals

Anyone can create a bypass trust, including people who are not married. In this case, the trust documents name the person who will serve as the life beneficiary. This person will receive the rights to the property to use during his or her lifetime. In addition, anyone can be named as a beneficiary to receive the property after the life beneficiary has passed on.

You might wish to use this method of leaving property if you want to allow someone to use your estate after you die but you want someone else to own the property outright after that time. It is important to point out that the life beneficiary cannot include your property in his or her estate at the time of death because he or she does not own the property outright. You should trust the person you name trustee to manage the property for you throughout this time.

Bypass Trusts for Unmarried Couples

What should you do to take advantage of these tax savings if you are part of an unmarried couple? The same type of tax savings from an AB trust can be obtained, but this type of trust is simply called a life estate trust. In addition, the marital deduction is not applicable to this type of trust. This does mean any amount of money you own at the time of your death over the personal exemption amount is taxable. The only way around this is to use a charitable trust, in which your property is given to a charity. The amount of tax savings for the unmarried couple is still significant, however.

Beneficiary for Single Individuals

Some single individuals will benefit from using the bypass trust just for the tax savings. For example, you might wish to leave your valuable estate to your cousin and name that cousin's children as your final beneficiaries. Your cousin will be able to receive your property at the time of your death as a life beneficiary to use that property as he or she needs to over the rest of his or her life or according to the terms you set forth in the trust. When the cousin dies, your estate goes to the children you named as final beneficiaries.

This might seem like an extra step, but because of the cost savings of a bypass trust, it is a good option for you to consider. Keep in mind that anything over the personal exemption amount for that year is still taxable.

To sum up, a bypass trust might be one of the best methods available to you to save on estate taxes. If you do have a valuable amount of property that you believe will withstand your lifetime and that of your spouse, you should protect that property from double taxation. Without a bypass trust, you could find your estate going through taxation at the time of your death as well as at the time of your beneficiary or spouse's death. It is best to consider a bypass trust if your property is valued over the personal exemption.

Establishing and Funding the Trust

Funding a trust simply means you will put property into the trust. Most forms of trusts allow you to add to them as you need to. The terms of the trust will outline what requirements there are. Remember, the creator of the trust establishes the terms for it. There are laws governing the rules on establishing trusts. Each state will have its own laws in place. In some states, you can establish a trust with just a dollar investment. The funds used to establish the trust are called the trust res or principal.

There are several ways to fund a trust. It can be funded partially at the time of establishment, or it can be funded later. It can also be funded with contingent funding — for example, with the proceeds from a life insurance policy. It can be funded with the assets that have gone through probate through the will when the creator dies. This is called a pour-over will. The assets from the will fund the trust.

Once the principal is in the trust, it can be invested to generate income and, like all income, it is taxable by the Internal Revenue Service. Some states also tax this income. The income from the trust remains in the trust if you have an irrevocable trust except as it is paid out to beneficiaries according to the trust terms.

Funding the trust is not just a good way to pass gifts on to beneficiaries, it is also a good way to manage your retirement.

How a Trust Works in Retirement

Many people use living trusts to aid them during their retirements. If they do not want to or become unable to manage their estates as they age, a trust allows someone else to step in and do it for them. For example, suppose Mary Ann and William are happily married with two grown children and three grandchildren. They have worked hard and have a home that is paid off, as well as stocks, bonds, and other investments. Their estate is valued at $500,000. They both have retirement accounts from their employers. They have established a living trust to allow someone else to help them manage their estate when they get older or no longer wish to do so.

A trust can have various features implemented to allow the creator to manage his or her estate. In the case of Mary Ann and William, there are various features they put in place in their trust. First, both Mary Ann and William will serve as joint trustees. They name their attorney the alternative trustee. Their attorney would be able to step in should both of them become incompetent or die at the same time. In addition, if they decide to resign as trustees, the attorney can step in place for them.

The income generated from the trust is paid to Mary Ann and William. The principal is available to them to use as they would like to. They can add to the trust or take assets from it as they deem necessary. They can continue to use the trust as long as they would like to. The trust can be revoked at any time until the survivor becomes incompetent or dies.

Mary Ann and William have determined they will avoid probate on much of their estate. To do this, they need to add their assets to the trust. To add them, they simply need to change the legal document to represent ownership of the property. This includes their stocks and bonds, their home, and their other assets.

For other items, such as household property and vehicles, Mary Ann and William can also add them to the trust if they would like to. Doing so requires that any items sold, exchanged, or abandoned be accounted for. When adding any real or tangible property to a trust, keep in mind this requirement. It creates the need for a lot of paperwork management — too much for most people to handle. Therefore, some of these assets could be left out of the trust and passed on to beneficiaries through the will.

On the other hand, adding liquid assets such as stocks and bonds makes sense. It is easy enough to do by simply including the ownership of the property in the trust legal documents. It is advisable to work with your attorney in this process.

Designating the Trustee

A trust that does not have a named trustee will be invalid. Every state provides the trustee's responsibilities. The trust terms also define the tasks the trustee will perform or is able to perform.

As with selecting an executor of your will, you should invest time in selecting the right person to manage your trust. The person should be willing to do so and should also have the capacity for doing so. They might have to make critical decisions at some point. Take time to make a wise decision here; do not just select someone you feel obligated to pick.

The duties of a trustee often include administering the trust according to the terms. In other words, they have to follow the terms of the trust, which are put in place by the creator of the trust, and make sure those terms are carried out. They also might manage the property within the trust. This often includes reinvesting the assets in the trust in such a way that would be profitable for the trust. The principal of the trust is also invested.

The trustee must also take on the administrative duties regarding the trust. This includes maintaining accurate accounting records for the trust. The trustee needs to file taxes and make key tax decisions. At the time determined by the trust terms, the trustee also must move the trust property to the right beneficiaries. Throughout the time the trust owns the property, the trustee must have an accurate record of it. Then, when the property is transferred to the beneficiary, records can be used to verify what was moved and what happened to its value over the time the property was within the trust.

The final duty of the trustee is to close, or terminate, the trust. For example, the trust can be carried out for years after the creator's death to provide for children. The terms might state that the trust will give $50,000 to the child every year until the trust's funds are depleted. The trustee maintains the trust throughout that time, until the trust is no longer needed.

Who should have these duties? If the trust will be a revocable trust, you can name you and your spouse if you are married. This might be one of the best choices for a living trust of this nature.

Another route to take is to name two co-trustees. They would work together to administer the trust. For example, you could name someone close to you and whom you believe would carry out your wishes. The second trustee could be an institution. The institution will be in place for the long term, even after the other trustee has died.

Naming individuals as trustees

You might wish to name a friend or a relative to the trustee position. Before doing so, realize what the duties are and determine whether the individual can handle them in the long term. In addition, because trusts are not managed by the court system, it is possible for there to be some misappropriation.

One of the best ways to avoid the trustee or anyone else taking funds from the trust against your wishes is to hire a third-party accounting firm to handle a yearly accounting of the trust. The accounting firm should report directly to the beneficiaries you list for the trust. This can help you feel more comfortable about appointing individuals to the trustee position rather than an institution. In addition, you can also require the trustee to post bond to protect your beneficiaries. This is similar to requiring a will executor to post bond to protect beneficiaries from the loss of their inheritance.

Naming institutions as trustees

Appointing an institution as trustee is not uncommon. Find out about their fees for maintaining the trust. Most institutions do charge a fee, which is a percentage of the assets in the trust. Also, ask about the institution's investment policies. You will need to be in agreement on them. Learn who is likely to invest the money for your particular trust and talk with this person. You need to be comfortable with him or her. You can ask for references. At the same time, you want to do some research on the institution, too. For example, are there claims against their trust department? Do they have a high employee turnover? How experienced are their trust employees?

In addition, you need to protect your beneficiaries in the long term from poor management by an institution. Within the trust, allow beneficiaries to replace one institution with another. The beneficiaries are not usually able to take control of the trust themselves or put it in the hands of another individual, but they should be given the ability to move the trust from one institution to another. The initial institution might go out of business. Even worse, the beneficiaries might feel that the trust is being mismanaged by the institution and wish to move it. Adding this ability to the trust is as simple as including it in the trust terms.

CASE STUDY: A LOVED ONE'S EXPERIENCE

Lisa Capozzi
Los Angeles, California

Lisa Capozzi had never really had any experience with wills and estate planning until her father passed away. At 88 years old, he was in fairly good health, and his death was unexpected. Luckily, he had planned accordingly with an estate plan; unluckily, his family did not handle it well, and even today, problems still plague the family with the estate still up in the air.

"Five months ago my dad passed away unexpectedly," she said at the time of the interview. "He was still fairly active, driving his own car and traveling quite extensively. My six siblings and I knew he had some sort of written will, but we didn't really know how he had divided his assets.

"The difficult part of this process after his passing is that, for one, things seem to be moving at a snail's pace. Not only that, there is a huge communication gap between the beneficiaries — myself and my siblings — and the executors — my dad's accountant, a brother-in-law, and my dad's second wife. No one is informing us what is supposed to happen or what is happening."

Capozzi said this lack of communication was maddening and created a feeling of suspicion that either the money was being extorted or that fees for services and commissions on IRAs were mounting.

"This is very difficult, as we know the money my dad left for us is he and my mom's life's work," Capozzi added. "We're certain they would want us, not others, to benefit from all of their hard work." Capozzi said her father did not talk much about money while he was alive and was always a bit secretive about his finances and keeping her mom in the dark as well. "In his death, in a way, he continued his secretive ways regarding money," Capozzi said.

Capozzi has talked to countless attorneys and also performed an extensive amount of research on the Internet, but there still does not seem to be any answers. This is just one example of how important it is to have your will or trust planned out and understood by those among the living.

"There is extensive information about wills and trusts on the Internet and thousands of attorneys to contact, and yet I still don't know how to protect the assets my dad set aside for us," she explained. "I've finally seen a copy of the will and trust. Yet, how would I know for certain that it is being executed properly? I don't have a law or accounting degree. I don't have money to hire an attorney to look after my interests. I'm frustrated during this very sad time in my life when I have now lost both my parents. I know the money can't bring them back, but it would certainly help to ease the financial difficulties my husband and I are plagued with during these volatile economic times."

For Capozzi, she hopes a situation like this never happens to anyone else. "To anyone who has a will, share specifically what you have and what you are leaving to whom before you pass on," she advised. "It's pretty difficult to read your mind after you've died. If communication with your loved ones about your will is not possible, then at least leave specific directions for your accountant and/or attorney about the timeframe and methods for the execution of your will. The extra step will avoid frustration and stress for your loved ones."

One Final Note on Wills and Trusts

There are many other types of trusts available that can work in conjunction with your will. You can use a trust as a way of passing property to charities or even for skipping generations to benefit your grandchildren rather than your children. It is important to work with an estate planning attorney to help you to create the right type of trust for your particular needs. Keep in mind that most goals can be met, but you must do so within the confines of the law if you hope for your will to stand up in court and with the IRS.

Chapter 12

Medical Decisions
and Incapacity

Many people often do not make arrangements for what should happen if they are in the hospital and unable to make their own decisions. This leaves the decisions to family members who can either substitute their own ideas or guess what the patient would want to be done (or not done).

As has been previously mentioned, there are legal mechanisms you can use to keep such medical decisions in your own hands if you wish. You can also arrange for someone of your choosing to handle your financial affairs on your behalf.

A will is traditionally used to make your wishes known after you die. However, in a true estate plan, you can also plan for situations when you are unable to make decisions for a period during your lifetime, sometimes a long period, due to your physical or mental inability. A durable power of attorney can cover both health care decisions and financial matters. A more limited durable power of attorney for health care can be prepared to cover health care decisions on your behalf, as well as a living will, advance directive for health care, or health care proxy — depending on which mechanism is recognized in your state or best for your purpose. Although none of these documents dispose of assets by gift or bequest, they pertain to significant life decisions and have a place in your estate plan.

Medical Decisions

Medical decisions are usually a person's primary concern. Medical advances have enabled people to live longer, including by life-sustaining medical technology. Not all people have welcomed the result of these advances because staying alive does not always equate with quality living. Thus, many people worry their lives will be sustained longer than they want by machine. On the other hand, others embrace such technology as a means of living long enough to be cured of a terminal condition. You might be interested in the right to die with your dignity intact, or you might be interested in prolonging your life by any means available. Whichever choice is yours, a living will or equivalent document makes your wishes clear and enforceable.

Right-to-die laws in this country are controversial. Changes in this area of law are likely to continue. It is important for you to consider the fact that at the time of this writing, the U.S. Supreme Court and all state legislatures have upheld the right of a patient to die with dignity instead of being kept alive through artificial means according to the patient's wishes. In addition to this, the Supreme Court has also stated that an individual has the right to control the amount and type of medical treatment he or she receives. Medical personnel have to follow "clear and convincing evidence" of the person's wishes to die without intervention, to have his or her life sustained, or to give someone else the power to make this decision for him or her. Federal law requires hospitals and care facilities that receive Medicare and Medicaid funds to honor living wills and their equivalents whether their state law recognizes them or not.

Do you need to put your wishes in writing? Many people are content that their family will do all that they can and make the right decisions based on their beliefs. However, if you want to ensure your beliefs and wishes will prevail, it should be important to you to include these beliefs and wishes in your estate plan.

Each state allows individuals to create documents that outline their wishes for medical care or at the least designate someone to make these decisions in their stead. Although you might be able to do this for yourself in a simple letter, the better approach is to work with your attorney to draft a proper document. These documents contain your specific directions to be followed whenever you cannot make your own decisions about critical medical procedures or life sustaining methods. Most of these documents do not become relevant unless you are in a coma or have been diagnosed with a terminal condition. In other words, they are not used every time you visit the doctor. Further, so long as you are able to communicate your wishes for yourself and are legally capable of making those decisions, these documents are not needed.

One of the key benefits of creating these documents is that they can relieve your family members from having to make difficult decisions for you at a stressful time. This can make the situation easier for them and enable you to still maintain some control over your life. Some of your family members might have different opinions and thoughts than you do about the subject of the right to die. Also, in some situations, medical personnel might not follow the instruction of your family member(s) if they believe another course of action is the best option for you. Your own directive requires medical personnel to follow your wishes.

Advance health care directives

As has been previously mentioned in Chapter 2, all but four states expressly recognize living wills or advance directives for health care. Some states provide forms for these documents by statute. It is important to employ the terminology used in your state when preparing your advance directive for health care or living will. There are many decisions you can make within an advance health care directive. The goal is to list what you want and do not want in terms of health care if you are seriously ill and unable to speak for yourself at the time care is being rendered. Each state defines the circumstances that trigger the applicability of such a directive, but common features are the patient's terminal condition, brain death, or indefinite vegetative state, with incompetency to communicate. *A sample advance directive for health care is included in Appendix C for illustrative purpose.*

There are some types of care that are more commonly addressed by these directives than others. The following are some items you might wish to address in your advance directive for health care:

- Blood and blood-related product use
- Dialysis
- Drug use
- Diagnostic testing
- Cardiopulmonary resuscitation (CPR) to get your heart back to pumping
- Respirator use to keep your lungs working artificially

- Use of feeding tube
- Surgical procedures that might help extend your life
- Any other extraordinary means of maintaining life support you may wish to identify

You can also use your advance health care directive to make decisions about your desires for other types of care that could be administered to you while you are incapacitated. These include food, water, and medications used for pain management. The laws in many states allow medical personnel to administer pain medication because the assumption is that most people do not want to be in agony during serious, life-threatening instances.

Washington state has an example of a progressive law. Washington's Death with Dignity Act provides that a resident of the state who is competent and at least age 18, and who has been determined by the attending and consulting physicians to be suffering from a terminal disease, can voluntarily express his or her wish to die and make a written request for medication to self-administer to end his or her life in a humane and dignified manner. Oregon has a similar law. There are stringent procedural requirements built into the "assisted suicide" laws, and medical providers are not required to dispense the requested drugs if they are against it. You cannot set up such a situation for yourself in advance of being in the imminent situation. Although you cannot yet direct "assisted" death in advance by proxy or living will, these laws evidence an emergent public policy that honors an individual's right to make these ultimate life decisions.

In instances where you do not want your life prolonged in any way, you might want to include a statement in your health care directive that specifically says you want all pain relief, food, and water withheld from you. By federal law, you are able to impose these types of instructions in your health care directive even if your state does not recognize specific procedures in these situations.

Durable powers of attorney, designation of proxy or surrogate

Another vehicle for handling medical decisions and other matters if you become incompetent to do so for yourself is the durable power of attorney. In this document, you can designate another person, your attorney in fact (who does not have to be a lawyer), to act for you. By power of attorney, you give this person the ability to stand in your shoes for making decisions. A broad durable power of attorney can authorize your attorney in fact to not only direct medical care for you but also handle all your other affairs. By its terms, the document states that its power survives your incapacity, which means it is "durable." If it does not have such a provision, the power of attorney will lapse when you become incompetent. A durable power of attorney for health care can designate an attorney in fact, a proxy, or a surrogate — depending on the term used by your state for only decisions related to your medical condition and related health care. Whether it is a general durable power of attorney or a durable power of attorney for health care, be sure the person you appoint is someone who will express your wishes. Discuss your desires and goals thoroughly with this person in advance. *A sample durable power of attorney is included in Appendix C for illustrative purpose.*

Just because you make these statements does not mean they will be followed. When you make such decisions, be sure your attorney in fact is able to understand what your true wishes are and will be able to advocate them for you. There might be a time when he or she must fight for you to accomplish this.

Of course, the opposite of this position is also true. If you want to ensure you are given all the medical attention you need, including food, pain medication, and water, you can make this a specific aspect of a health care directive. You can leave such wishes in your directive, and they will be honored. In fact, you should do this any time you have strong feelings one way or the other about prolonging life.

If you are unsure of what types of procedures you do and do not want, make an appointment with your physician to talk about these procedures. He or she can give you an honest, third-party explanation to help you make such decisions. You might wish to bring your attorney in fact with you so he or she understands your wishes.

Even as you express your wishes in these documents, you still might find your family has to make some decisions for you. You can add the following aspects to your health care directive if you also have strong feelings about them:

1. When should any type of medical treatment be withheld? For example, how long should you be incapacitated before you wish the treatment to be stopped?

2. Should pain medication or medication to treat infections be used to prolong your life or reduce your pain?

3. Should expensive, risky surgeries be performed if they could prolong your life? Specifically, you might want to consider what would happen if a procedure was available that could help to prolong your life if the procedure would not aid in reversing the medical condition keeping you incapacitated.

There might be other decisions someone will need to make when you are incapacitated that you have not covered in your health care directive. In these situations, your attorney in fact will need to be able to make key decisions for you based on your specific needs. Your health care directive can specifically state the decisions this person can and cannot make. For those who wish to have more control, you might want to specifically outline the decisions the attorney in fact can make.

When does a health care directive become effective?

Health care directives go into effect when you cannot make decisions for yourself because you lack the capacity to make those decisions. This can be interpreted several ways. First, if you cannot understand the nature of the decisions you are being asked to make, this could trigger the directive to be used. Second, you might be unable to communicate your wishes. Communication might be done by orally stating your wishes or in other ways such as through gestures or in writing.

In any situation where you cannot express your wishes in any way because you are comatose or extremely injured, the health care directive should take precedence. It is important to note that just because you have made the health care directive effective immediately does not mean your attorney in fact is able to override anything you have included in your declaration. You still have the ability to make your own decisions through the declaration. Your attorney in fact must make decisions that correlate with your declarations.

Durable power of attorney

The durable power of attorney can be created in two ways. One way allows you to put it into play right away. In other words, once the document is organized and laid out, it is in place and serving you. The second option is to allow the durable power of attorney to be set up but not put into effect until a certain time. Generally, this is when your doctor decides you are incapacitated and therefore cannot make sound decisions yourself. You can select the document that is right for your situation.

There are some situations that will require you to make a durable power of attorney effective right away. For example, you might be ill or you might know your health is on the decline. Once you state when the document goes into effect, your attorney in fact has the ability to assist with your financial decisions and managing your funds. Many people do not want someone to just take over, but they do want someone there just in case there comes a time when they are unable to make decisions for themselves. You could make the durable power of attorney effective immediately, but you must trust the person you name attorney in fact will not use his or her powers until necessary.

If you do decide to keep your attorney in fact in the background to be called into service only when there is a need, such as if you become incapacitated, you can use what is called a springing power of attorney. This just means the durable power of attorney is not effective, and the attorney in fact is not empowered to act unless a doctor determines you are unable to make decisions for yourself. This process is not always an easy one. For example, if you are involved in a car accident and fall into a coma, the attorney in fact will need to go through doctors to get statements of your incapacity before he or she can act on your behalf. This process can take some time. If you plan to create a springing power of attorney, it is best to have your attorney prepare it for you.

Now that you have a good idea what this type of document can do for you and have made some decisions, the next step is to make sure the durable power of attorney is legally binding. This is not a document to be created from a generic form or without assistance of legal counsel, as state laws can vary. For example, not all states require these documents be signed in front of a notary public, though it is always a good idea to do this. In those states that do not require it, there will likely be a requirement of witnesses on the document, similar to a will.

If your durable power of attorney specifically gives the attorney in fact control over real estate, you must record or register this with your land records office, usually a county office. This must be done in any county in which you own property. If you are putting a springing power of attorney in place, the document does not have to be filed until the durable power of attorney goes into effect. At minimum, your attorney in fact should have the power of attorney in hand.

It is also important to avoid naming your doctor as your attorney-in-fact. Your doctor should be the person that your attorney in fact consults with when making health care decisions about you. Most state laws prohibit your doctor from serving the role of attorney in fact.

Financial Decisions

Medical decisions are an important part of your estate plan, but financial decisions are also important. In the last years of your life, you might find yourself in a position where you need to consider managing your finances through someone else. You might become unable to make important decisions, or you simply might no longer want to have to worry about your finances. When something like this happens, you will want to have some type of plan in place.

The decisions you can make using a health care directive are similar to those you can make for your financial situation. You will again use an attorney in fact who becomes your durable power of attorney for your finances. Every state allows you to do so. This person can be anyone you want, including your spouse, a good friend, or a relative.

If you do not prepare a durable power of attorney, a family member will need to petition the court to have him or her elected as such. This process is called a conservatorship or guardianship proceeding. It is important to note that this process is time consuming, and it can be a bit more complex than initiating a health care directive. It is expensive, too. The durable power of attorney, though, is a rather simplistic process that allows you to establish your wishes ahead of time, which makes it far easier for someone to take control over your finances if the need arises.

The most complex aspect of this process is choosing someone you trust to make decisions for you. The best way to protect your assets is to include specific directions in your durable power of attorney so there is little question about what your wishes are. This makes the job of the attorney in fact much easier. In most situations, the attorney in fact will have the authority to manage most financial matters considered "routine," such as paying your bills. If you wish for this person to do something more than this for you, you will need to explicitly state that in your document.

Even if you list a variety of situations and how you wish for the attorney in fact to handle them, it is still important to choose someone you trust because it is unlikely you will be able to predict all possible situations you might face and their possible outcomes. This person should be a good financial judge, and he or she should be willing to do the job. You might even name the same person as your attorney in fact for your health care directives and your financial management. If you name two people for these positions, the two are likely to have to work together to make some decisions, so be sure they can do so.

In some situations, you might wish to pay your attorney in fact for helping you manage your finances. If you want this to happen, simply state it within the document. Most often, this is not necessary because it is simplistic enough. However, if you plan to have this person manage a number of investments, you might wish to compensate him or her for doing so.

What can the attorney in fact do for you?

There are a variety of decisions that your attorney in fact can make for you. It is up to you to decide what you would like this individual to control. Specify this in the document. Some of the tasks you might wish to consider include:

- Use your savings and checking accounts to pay standard bills, including utilities

- Cash checks or deposit them into your accounts for you

- Handle transactions with your bank or other investment organizations with which you do business

- Pay your taxes, manage your mortgage, buy property, and sell property for you, both commercial and residential

- Invest your funds into stocks, bonds, or other investments as you so choose

- Collect all benefits made to you, including those from social security, Medicare, and other accounts

- Represent you in a court of law

- Help you to hire employees, fire employees, or otherwise manage your business

- Buy and sell, cancel, or pay for your insurance products

- File your income taxes or other tax obligations

- Manage your retirement investment accounts

The durable power of attorney will give your attorney in fact the ability to do all of these things. It is important to note, though, that he or she will need to show documentation of this right to any of facilities that request it; otherwise, he or she might be unable to proceed with such transactions.

Even though you are giving your attorney in fact so many abilities, he or she cannot make decisions he or she feels are best. Rather, this individual needs to make decisions that correspond with the details and directions you leave for him or her.

Signing, dating, and storing

Now that you have the document organized, what do you do with it? You should alert your attorney in fact of the document's location — though he or she should have his or her own copy. Be aware that some people will not want to take on this task because it implies he or she might have to make tough decisions that are life altering for you. This is not the type of thing you want to throw at them at the last minute. In addition to your attorney in fact, you should also keep a copy with your doctor, a good friend, and your attorney.

There are various locations where you can get the health care directives, declarations, and power of attorney documents. You can find these through your attorney, of course, or you might be able to obtain them through other sources such as the Internet, your local library, or even your doctor or hospital. Although it is recommended you consult with your attorney about any complex aspects of these papers, there is really no need to involve the attorney if you just want a simple document outlining your wishes. Those with straightforward wishes can find health care directive documents at some senior centers, the state's medical association, and various office supply stores selling legal documents. The AARP is great source for more information and for document options. You can visit the organization's website at **www.aarp.org** to obtain downloadable documents.

Once you have the documents outlined and organized, it is time to sign them. As you know from creating your will, it is critical to have your documents appropriately signed and dated with witnesses. Each state requires that you sign these documents stating you understand what they contain and that they are accurate representations of what you wish to happen. In some situations, you can direct another person to sign them for you, such as if you are unable to physically sign them. It is best to have these signed in front of a notary public to ensure the documents are valid should they be contested.

Keep in mind you do have to keep these documents updated. You might want to change your documents if you move out of state, if your wishes change, or if you believe your attorney in fact is no longer capable of performing his or her duties. Take the time to gather all other copies of the document to have them destroyed. In addition, note that any details in these documents can be changed. The only time this will be contested is if there is some reason to believe you are no longer of sound mind to make such decisions.

CASE STUDY:
ADVICE FROM A
COURT ADMINISTRATOR

Steven D. Fields
Probate Court Two
Fort Worth, TX

Steven Fields, a court administrator/senior administrative attorney in Fort Worth, Texas, Probate Court Two, has been working with will and probate for the past 22 years and has seen much during that time.

For all the stories, he believes a person should definitely have a will before they die; there is never any reason not to at least have something written down. In Texas, handwritten wills are legal, too.

"It needs to be dispositive, which means it shows the decedent intended to give his or her property to the person named in the will, and it must either be all in the handwriting of and signed by the decedent or be signed by the decedent and two witnesses," he said.

The most important thing he believes a person should remember when putting together a will or creating an estate plan is to name only one independent executor at a time and make sure you name contingent beneficiaries in case your residuary beneficiary predeceases you.

"Naming co-executors is never a good idea, as they often disagree, which ends up using estate funds to pay attorneys to resolve the dispute," he said.

Adding to that thought, he emphasized, "[Name] one person! How many people can drive a car at the same time?"

Even though it might be likely that you would want to name one of your children as an executor or power of attorney, Fields cautioned against this in some cases. "When children are competitive and naming one would infuriate the others," would be one example when this would not be advisable.

When determining a power of attorney or choosing an executor for your will, "A court cannot appoint an executor who has been convicted of a felony," Fields noted. "Although you can, you should not name an agent under a power of attorney who has been convicted of a felony. You need to implicitly trust the person you name as an agent under a power of attorney or as executor. He or she needs to be good with money and good at making reasonable, thoughtful decisions and needs to be able to treat all beneficiaries fairly."

As for naming a power of attorney, keep in mind what this means overall. "Under a financial power of attorney, a person names an agent to step into his or her shoes to make the transactions described in the power of attorney," Fields said. "A durable financial power of attorney continues to be valid even after a person becomes incapacitated. Before selling real property, the power of attorney must be filed in the deed records of the county where the real property is located. A durable power of attorney expires upon the death of the person executing the power of attorney."

Chapter 13

Final Life Decisions

ost of the work of creating a will has been completed, but before you sit back, it is necessary to consider a few more aspects of this process. Specifically, you need to consider whether you are interested in making decisions regarding your body, organ donation, and any final arrangements you would like to have organized.

Some people state that this is the job of their loved ones. They do not want to have to think about these aspects. Other people are interested in being a part of these decisions. They want to alleviate the entire burden from their loved ones' shoulders. The choice is yours, as there is no rule that states your estate plan should include this information.

You Are in Charge of Your Decisions

Think back to a time when someone close to you died. You were grief stricken and unable to think of a life without this person.

Yet, if you were put in the position to make immediate decisions, could you do so? For some who have been in this position, there is a desire to prevent anyone else from having to guess what their wishes were.

Some of the important decisions you will have to deal with include deciding whether your organs should be donated and whether you want to be buried or cremated. These are just a few of the things you can plan for, however. These are decisions you can make for yourself now so your family does not have to worry about them, plan for them, or even worse, pay for them. Think about how your decisions now will affect your family when you die. For example, deciding you do not want any type of funeral might crush family members who wish to come together to celebrate your life. It is often best to include these individuals in your decisions or at least talk to them about those decisions.

The following are some areas where you might specifically want to consider leaving directions in your will or as part of your estate plan:

- **Donation of body parts:** Many people have specific ideas and thoughts on organ donation that they want honored. If you do donate organs, keep in mind you will still need to make arrangements for the rest of your body, such as cremation or burial.

- **Donation of body to science:** In order for your body to be donated to science, you will have to make arrangements for this process before you die. It cannot be done for you after death. If you wish to do this, the body is most often cremated after students study it. The remains can then be buried or scattered. Your family might request that the body be sent to them for burial, and they should be notified that it might take a considerable amount of time — in some cases up to a year — to transport your body back to them for burial. Also, keep in mind that there are often limited instances when a body can be donated. If you die in a way that prevents science from using your remains, your family will need to seek other alternatives for you. For example, extreme bodily trauma might leave your body unusable. In this situation, it is important that you explain how you wish your body to be disposed.

- **Funerals:** You might want to outline your wishes for your funeral. Although it might be a difficult decision to ponder, it is important to consider this. You might want to have a traditional ceremony in a funeral home, or you might want to have a simple celebration rather than a sad funeral. You might also have specific wishes regarding embalming, or you might want to be cremated. These are all aspects you can prepare for through your will.

For those who believe there is simply no reason to have to worry about any of these things, think about this: You have likely designed your estate plan to help your family save thousands of dollars in estate taxes. Why would you like them to throw that all away on a funeral you really do not want them to have? You can help your family save money by giving you what you want rather than what they think they have to do.

Making Your Wishes Known

After you have thought about your wishes, you will need to get them in writing. In some situations, you might be able to simply make your wishes known and trust that your family will have no problem carrying them out for you. On the other hand, it might be important for you to leave it in writing.

Most states have laws that require written instructions left by the deceased concerning how his or her body is to be honored. This is also generally the case even where such laws are not in place. You can include these written instructions within your will. Although doing this is legal, do not make this the only place your wishes are made known. A will is not often readily available immediately after your death when such decisions are made. In some cases, it can take weeks or longer for a will to be found. Meanwhile, it only takes a few hours before decisions have to be made for your body, especially if you are donating your organs or your body to science.

What if you do nothing, if you do not leave any wishes, or if they are not found in time? Your next of kin will make the decision for you regarding what will happen. This can be a spouse or a child, in most cases.

Considering Other Wishes

You might have other wishes concerning aspects of your death. The following sections detail other aspects you might want to consider.

Death notices

Do you want to write your own death notice? Many people do this because they want to ensure those who mean the most to them are noted. A death notice is almost always done within a day or so of the individual's death, so it is something your family will need to do right away if you do not write it.

You can write your own death notice, but most of the information provided will greatly depend on when you die, how you will be celebrated, and so on. Therefore, some of the work must be done by your family. Still, you can write these details out for your family, get everyone's name right, and even make arrangements for payment so your family does not have to deal with this.

If you want to take this one step farther, you can write your own obituary, which provides many more details of your life. By writing your own obituary, you can include what you want people to know about you or remember about you. You do not have to do this, but if you feel your thoughts need to be heard, or if you just want it done your own way, there is no reason not to do so. The obituary might be something you want submitted to the local paper for publication, distributed to an alma mater, or simply sent to family and friends. Be sure to include any specific instructions for what should be done with the document after your death.

Ceremony planning

If you have specific wishes for your funeral, you can simply make your wishes known through a document you leave behind. You can go into as much or as little detail as you would like. Simple funerals, lying-in states, and memorial services need to be planned for by someone if they are to happen. The following are several ways that you can take care of this yourself:

1. Plan your services in advance on your own. You can do this by writing out your plans and including them with your other wishes. If you do this, you will need to keep in mind that someone will have to make sure everything can happen and prepare the formal arrangements at the time

of death. It might be expensive, too, which means you might want to make plans in your will to cover these costs.

2. You could work with a funeral director to plan your services to prepay and preplan for your funeral needs. These services are actually becoming more common as more people want to be in control of their lives and deaths. This also allows you to pay for all of your expenses ahead of time, so you do not have to worry about family members having to pay for them.

After you have made your decisions, it is best to talk with your family about them. It is imperative that they not only know what your plans are, but also that they have some say in how they remember you after you die. If you have any other specific directions for after your death, you can leave them behind in your will. So long as there are funds to cover them and no laws are violated in the process, your last wishes should be met.

Conclusion

Although obtaining legal counsel and assistance of other knowledgeable estate planning experts is important, you should be the architect of your will. Once you have an understanding of your specific circumstances now and your future projections, you can approach an estate plan with thoughtful understanding.

The information provided in this book gives you tools to draft your own basic will and to outline other elements of an estate plan to pursue with experts. You can also use the information in each section to help you to obtain documents to assist you.

If you need additional help, consider using the following resources.

- AARP is a great source of information, tips, and resources for anyone who is creating a will or estate plan. You can visit the organization's website at **www.aarp.org** to find most of what you need.

- The IRS provides information and guidance on estate and gift taxes. This is the best resource for current limits, exemptions, and trust law changes. If you have a tax question regarding your estate planning, the IRS website (**www.irs.gov**) is filled with useful information. You can also contact the IRS through its local offices.

- Your own state bar association.

When you have worked through the preparatory process for creating a will and estate plan, step back and give yourself some time to think. What is the best method for passing your estate and assets on to future generations? Are you satisfied with your planning? Have you discussed your planning with your spouse?

Finally, remember to keep your documents in a safe place accessible to people who will need them if you are ill and when you die. This includes your spouse, attorney in fact, legal counsel, and executor. You should also review your will and estate plan annually to keep current with your own desires and circumstances as well as any changes in the law.

Appendix A

Estate Planning Worksheets

Property Ownership Inventory — What to Include in Your Will

This worksheet will assist you in itemizing your assets to give you a complete picture of everything you own. Using this worksheet, you can better determine specific bequests you might wish to make to individuals as well as understand what will become part of the residue of your probate estate under your will.

Real estate ownership:

Description of property:

_____

_____

_____

_____

_____

_____

_____

List each parcel of real estate owned according to individual deeds, including the address of the property, the current value (along with the date), the price paid at the time of purchase (and date of purchase), any mortgage current in place on the property, and how the property is currently owned.

Financial account ownership:

_____

_____

_____

_____

_____

_____

Be sure to include all bank accounts, account numbers to identify them, the location of the accounts, the current values, and the names associated with each account.

Business ownership or interest:

_____

_____

_____

_____

_____

_____

List all details of any business ownership stake you might have, including sole proprietorships, partnerships, corporations, limited liability partnerships, and limited liability companies. Include the type of business, its name, its current value, ownership, and the value of the property to you.

Financial investment ownership:

_____

_____

_____

_____

_____

_____

List any financial investments, including all stocks, bonds, and other types of investments you own.

Retirement account ownership:

_____

_____

_____

_____

_____

Retirement accounts listed separately from other forms of investments. This will include any 401(k) ownership, IRAs, pension plans, or profit-sharing plans. List the account type, account number, the account owner, the beneficiaries you have listed with the investment firm, the value at the current date, and the location of the account. **Note that retirement accounts generally have a beneficiary designation that will pass proceeds outside of probate. Your estate can be a beneficiary, however. Consider how you want this asset to be handled and consult your attorney for options.**

Life insurance ownership:

_____

_____

_____

_____

_____

_____

_____

Life insurance is an asset if you currently own it. List the types of policies you have, as well as the company the insurance is with, the current value, the expiration date of the policy, the insured individual's name, and the beneficiary of any policy as you have listed with the insurance company. **Note that life insurance proceeds are not generally the subject of a will, but they can be. An example is having life insurance proceeds designated to fund a trust created in the will. Consult your attorney for options in this regard.**

Motor vehicles, boats, etc.

_____

_____

_____

_____

_____

_____

_____

_____

List cars, boats, RVs, motorcycles, trailers, 4-wheelers, snowmobiles, jet-skis, etc. titled in your name or otherwise your possession (some of these are not titled in all states).

Other assets

_____

_____

_____

_____

_____

_____

_____

_____

_____

_____

_____

_____

_____

List any additional assets you own. This can include all household items you plan to leave to someone in your will, including furniture, electronics, collections, sports equipment, vehicles, jewelry, and any item that has personal or monetary value.

Total asset value: _____

Updated: _____

Note: It is essential to update your inventory often, including any time you change ownership of an asset, gain or lose any significant value of assets, or when you acquire something new of value.

Family Pot Trust Worksheet

Use this form to outline your goals for using a family pot trust.

Name the children who are to be the beneficiaries of the family pot trust (add more lines if needed):

_____

_____

Trustee: _____

Successor trustee: _____

Property to be left in trust:

_____

_____

_____

_____

Special conditions:

Child's Property Guardian Worksheet

Use this for planning guardianship for your child/children — one guardian or multiple guardians options.

One property guardian for all your children:

_____
Property guardian

_____

Successor property guardian

Different property guardians for different children:

_____

Property guardian

For: _____

    Children's names

_____

_____

_____

Alternative property guardian for these children

_____

Property guardian

For: _____

    Children's names

_____

_____

_____

Alternative property guardian for these children

Note: You might also want to explain the reasons you made the choices you have regarding your guardianship choices; list these reasons, and feel free to make changes as you see fit.

Child's Trust Worksheet

In this section, you can list the important information for creating a trust for your children.

_____   _____

Child   Age at which trust
                                     terminates

_____

Trustee

_____

Successor trustee

Description of trust property:

_____
_____
_____
_____
_____

UTMA Custodians Worksheet

Use this section for planning and tracking gifts during your lifetime and by will to minors under the Uniform Transfers to Minors Act.

_____   _____

Child   Age child is to receive
                                                            gift (if state law lets
                                                            you choose the age)

_____

Custodian

_____

Alternate custodian

Description of UTMA specifications/property:

_____

_____

_____

_____

_____

Appendix B

State Statutes Related to Inheritance Rights of Posthumously Conceived Children

State	Citation	Relevant Portion of Statute
Alabama	Ala. Code §43-8-47	In order to inherit, the child must have been conceived prior to death of parent.
Alaska	Alaska Stat. §13-12-108	A child in gestation at decedent's death is treated as the decedent's child if the child survives for 120+ hours.
Arizona	Ariz. Rev. Stat. Ann § 14-2108	A child in gestation at decedent's death is treated as the decedent's child if the child survives for 120+ hours. In order to inherit, child must have been conceived prior to death of parent.
Arkansas	Ark. Code. Ann § 28-9-210	In order to inherit, the child must have been conceived prior to death of parent.
California	Cal. Probate Code §6407	A posthumous child may inherit if: (1) the decedent consented in writing to be treated as a parent; (2) if the decedent designated an agent; (3) the decedent's designated agent gives notice to the person with the power to control the distribution of the estate within four months of his death that the decedent's genetic material is available; and (4) a child is conceived within two years after the decedent's death.

State	Citation	Relevant Portion of Statute
Colorado	Colo. Rev. Stat. Ann. §15-11-108	Enacted §707, 9B ULA of the Uniform Parentage Act. Deceased parent is not treated as a parent of a posthumously conceived child unless he consented in a record to be a parent of such child.
Connecticut	N/A	No express statutory law.
Delaware	13 Del. C §8-707	Enacted §707, 9B ULA of the Uniform Parentage Act. Deceased parent is not treated as a parent of a posthumously conceived child unless he consented in a record to be a parent of such child. Posthumous children of intestate inherits are treated as if they were born during the decedent's lifetime.
Florida	Fla. Stat. Ann. §732.106, §742.17	A posthumously conceived child will not be eligible for a claim against the decedent's estate unless the child has been provided for by the decedent's will.
Georgia	Ga. Code Ann. §53-2.1(a)	In order to inherit, the child must have been conceived prior to death of parent.
Hawaii	Haw. Rev. Stat. §560:2-108	A child in gestation at decedent's death is treated as the decedent's child if the child survives for 120+ hours.
Idaho	Idaho Code §15-2-108	In order for the child to inherit as if born during the decedent's lifetime, the child must be conceived naturally or by artificial means before decedent's death but born within ten months after decedent's death.
Illinois	IL Code §755 art. 5 §2-3	Posthumous children of intestate inherits are treated as if they were born during the decedent's lifetime.
Indiana	IN Code §29-1-6-1 (51. Posthumous Children)	Posthumous children inherit as if born during the decedent's lifetime.
Iowa	IA Code Ann. §633.220	Posthumous children inherit as if born during the decedent's lifetime.
Kansas	KA Stat. Ann. §59-501	Posthumous children of intestate inherits are treated as if they were born during the decedent's lifetime.
Kentucky	KY Rev. Stat. Ann. §391.070	In order for a child to inherit as if born within decedent's lifetime, it must be born within ten months after decedent's death.

State	Citation	Relevant Portion of Statute
Louisiana	La. Civ. Code Ann. art. 940	A posthumously conceived child can inherit from a deceased parent if the decedent authorized in writing for the surviving spouse to use his genetic material for posthumous conception and the resulting child is born within three years of the decedent's death.
Maine	Me. Rev. Stat. Ann. tit. 18-A § 2-108	In order to inherit, the child must have been conceived prior to death of parent.
Maryland	Md. Ann. Code §3-107	In order to inherit, the child must have been conceived prior to death of parent.
Massachu-setts	Mass. Gen. Laws. Ann. 190 §8	Posthumous children of intestate inherits are treated as if they were born during the decedent's lifetime.
Michigan	Mich. Stat. Ann. §700.2108	A child in gestation at decedent's death is treated as the decedent's child if the child survives for 120+ hours.
Minnesota	Minn. Stat §542.2-108	A child in gestation at decedent's death is treated as the decedent's child if the child survives for 120+ hours.
Mississippi	N/A	No express statutory law.
Missouri	Ver. Ann. MI. Stat. §474.050	Posthumous children of intestate inherits are treated as if they were born during the decedent's lifetime.
Montana	Mont. Code Ann. §72-2-118	A child in gestation at decedent's death is treated as the decedent's child if the child survives for 120+ hours.
Nebraska	Neb. Rev. Stat. §30-2308	In order inherit, child must have been conceived prior to death of parent.
Nevada	Nev. Rev. Stat. Ann. §132.90	Posthumous children of intestate inherits are treated as if they were born during the decedent's lifetime.
New Hampshire	NH Rev. Stat. Ann §551:10	Posthumous children of intestate inherits are treated as if they were born during the decedent's lifetime. A father cannot deny a posthumous child of his or her right to inherit in a will.
New Jersey	N.J. Rev. Stat. Ann. §3B: 5-8	A child in gestation at decedent's death is treated as the decedent's child if the child survives for 120+ hours.
New Mexico	N.M. Stat. Ann §45-2-108	A child in gestation at decedent's death is treated as the decedent's child if the child survives for 120+ hours.
New York	N.Y. Estates, Powers and Trusts Law Section 2-1.3	In order to inherit, the child must have been conceived prior to death of parent.

State	Citation	Relevant Portion of Statute
North Carolina	N.C. Gen. Stat. Ann. §31-5.5	In order for a child to inherit as if born within decedent's lifetime, the child must be born within ten months after decedent's death.
North Dakota	N.D. Cent. Code §30.1-04-04	Enacted §707, 9B ULA of the Uniform Parentage Act. Deceased parent is not treated as a parent of a posthumously conceived child unless he consented in a record to be a parent of such child.
Ohio	OH Rev. Code Ann. §2105.14	Posthumous children inherit as if born during the decedent's lifetime.
Oklahoma	OK Stat. Ann. §228	Posthumous children of intestate inherits are treated as if they were born during the decedent's lifetime.
Oregon	Or. Rev. Stat. §112.075	In order to inherit, the child must have been conceived prior to death of parent.
Pennsylvania	PA Stat. Cons. Stat. Ann. §2104	Posthumous children inherit as if born during the decedent's lifetime.
Rhode Island	R.I. Gen. Laws. §§33-6-23, 33-6-24, 33-6-27	Posthumous children of intestate inherits are treated as if they were born during the decedent's lifetime.
South Carolina	Code Laws S.C. Ann. §27-5-120	In order for a child to inherit as if born during a decedent's lifetime, the child must be conceived before decedent's death and born within ten months of decedent's death.
South Dakota	S.D. Codified Laws Ann. §29A-2-108	A child in gestation at decedent's death is treated as the decedent's child if the child survives for 120+ hours.
Tennessee	Tenn. Code. Ann. §31-2-108	In order to inherit, the child must have been conceived prior to death of parent.
Texas	Tex. Fam. Code §160.707	Enacted §707, 9B ULA of the Uniform Parentage Act. Deceased parent is not treated as a parent of a posthumously conceived child unless he consented in a record to be a parent of such child. Posthumous children of intestate inherits are treated as if they were born during the decedent's lifetime.
Utah	Utah Code Ann. § 7-2-108	Enacted §707, 9B ULA of the Uniform Parentage Act. Deceased parent is not treated as a parent of a posthumously conceived child unless he consented in a record to be a parent of such child.
Vermont	N/A	No express statutory law.

State	Citation	Relevant Portion of Statute
Virginia	Va. Code Ann. §20-158B Va. Code. Ann. §20-164(i)	Deceased parent is not a parent of a posthumously conceived child unless implantation occurs before the treating physician can reasonably be advised of the decedent's death or the decedent parent consented in writing before implantation to be treated as a parent.
Washington	Rev. Code Wash. (ARCW) §26.26.730	Enacted §707, 9B ULA of the Uniform Parentage Act. Deceased parent is not treated as a parent of a posthumously conceived child unless he consented in a record to be a parent of such child. Posthumous children of intestate inherits are treated as if they were born during the decedent's lifetime.
West Virginia	W.Va. Code §421-8, §42-1-3f	A child in gestation at decedent's death is treated as the decedent's child if the child survives for 120+ hours.
Wisconsin	Wis. Stat. Ann. §854.21(5)	In order to inherit, the child must have been conceived prior to death of parent.
Wyoming	Wyo. Stat. §2-4-103	Enacted §707, 9B ULA of the Uniform Parentage Act. Deceased parent is not treated as a parent of a posthumously conceived child unless he consented in a record to be a parent of such child.

Appendix C

Sample Durable Power of Attorney for Health Care and Advance Directive (Living Will)

ote: These documents are provided for illustrative purposes. Consult your attorney to prepare a durable power of attorney and/or living will suitable for your own desires and circumstances and for legal enforceability in your state and/or in any state in which you are likely to receive health care.

Durable Power of Attorney for Health Care

It is important to choose someone to make health care decisions for you when you cannot make or communicate decisions for yourself. Tell the person you choose which health care treatments you want. The person you choose will be your agent. He or she will have the right to make decisions regarding your health care.

If you DO NOT choose someone to make decisions for you, write NONE on the line for the agent's name.

I,_____,SS#_____
(optional), appoint the person named in this document to be my agent to make my health care decisions.

This document is a durable power of attorney for health care decisions. My agent's power shall not end if I become incapacitated or if there is uncertainty that I am dead. This document revokes any prior durable power of attorney for health care decisions. My agent may not appoint anyone else to make decisions for me. My agent and caregivers are protected from any claims based on following this durable power of attorney for health care. My agent shall not be responsible for any costs associated with my care. I give my agent full power to make all decisions for me about my health care, including the power to direct the withholding or withdrawal of life-prolonging treatment, including artificially supplied nutrition and hydration/tube feeding. My agent is authorized to:

- Consent, refuse, or withdraw consent to any care, procedure, treatment, or service to diagnose, treat, or maintain a physical or mental condition, including artificial nutrition and hydration;

- Permit, refuse, or withdraw permission to participate in federally regulated research related to my condition or disorder;

- Make all necessary arrangements for any hospital, psychiatric treatment facility, hospice, nursing home, or other health care organization and employ or discharge health care personnel (any person authorized or permitted by the laws of the state to provide health care services) as he or she shall deem necessary for my physical, mental, or emotional well being;

- Request, receive, review, and authorize sending any information regarding my physical or mental health or my personal affairs, including medical and hospital records, and execute any releases that may be required to obtain such information;

- Move me into or out of any state or institution;

- Take legal action, if needed;

- Make decisions about autopsy, tissue, and organ donation, and the disposition of my body in conformity with state law; and

- Become my guardian if one is needed.

In exercising this power, I expect my agent to be guided by my directions as we discussed them prior to this appointment and/ or to be guided by my health care directive (see reverse side).

If you DO NOT want the person (agent) you name to be able to do one or other of the above things, draw a line through the statement and put your initials at the end of the line.

Agent's name: _____ Phone: _____

E-mail: _____

Address:_____

If you do not want to name an alternate, write "none."

Alternate agent's name: _____ Phone: _____
E-mail: _____
Address:_____

Execution and Effective Date of Appointment

My agent's authority is effective immediately for the limited purpose of having full access to my medical records and to confer with my health care providers and me about my condition. My agent's authority to make all health care and related decisions for me is effective when, and only when, I cannot make my own health care decisions.

SIGN HERE for the durable power of attorney and/or health care directive forms. Many states require notarization. It is recommended for the residents of all states. Please ask two persons to witness your signature who are not related to you or financially connected to your estate.

Signature: _____
Date: _____

Witness: _____
Date: _____

Witness: _____
Date: _____

Notarization:

On this _____ day of_____, in the year of _____, personally appeared before me the person signing, known by me to be the person who completed this document and acknowledged it as his or her free act and deed. IN WITNESS WHEREOF, I have set my hand and affixed my official seal in the County

of_____, State of _____, on
the date written above.

Notary Public: _____

Commission expires: _____

North Carolina GS 90-321 Statutory Form

Advance Directive for a Natural Death ("Living Will")

NOTE: YOU SHOULD USE THIS DOCUMENT TO GIVE YOUR HEALTH CARE PROVIDERS INSTRUCTIONS TO WITHHOLD OR WITHDRAW LIFE PROLONGING MEASURES IN CERTAIN SITUATIONS. THERE IS NO LEGAL REQUIREMENT THAT ANYONE EXECUTE A LIVING WILL.

GENERAL INSTRUCTIONS: You can use this Advance Directive ("Living Will") form to give instructions for the future if you want your health care providers to withhold or withdraw life prolonging measures in certain situations. You should talk to your doctor about what these terms mean. The Living Will states what choices you would have made for yourself if you were able to communicate. Talk to your family members, friends, and others you trust about your choices. Also, it is a good idea to talk with professionals such as your doctors, clergypersons, and lawyers before you complete and sign this Living Will.

You do not have to use this form to give those instructions, but if you create your own Advance Directive, you need to be careful to ensure it is consistent with North Carolina law.

This Living Will form is intended to be valid in any jurisdiction in which it is presented, but places outside North Carolina may impose requirements this form does not meet.

If you want to use this form, you must complete it, sign it, and have your signature witnessed by two qualified witnesses and proved by a notary public. Follow the instructions about which choices you can initial very carefully. Do not sign this form until two witnesses and a notary public are present to watch you sign it. You then should consider giving a copy to your primary physician and/or a trusted relative and should consider filing it with the Advanced Health Care Directive Registry maintained by the North Carolina Secretary of State: **www.nclifelinks.org**.

My Desire for a Natural Death

I, _____, being of sound mind, desire that, as specified below, my life not be prolonged by life prolonging measures:

1. When My Directives Apply

My directions about prolonging my life shall apply IF my attending physician determines I lack capacity to make or communicate health care decisions and:

NOTE: YOU MAY INITIAL ANY AND ALL OF THESE CHOICES.

_____
(Initial)

I have an incurable or irreversible condition that will result in my death within a relatively short period of time.

_____
(Initial)

I become unconscious and my health care providers determine that, to a high degree of medical certainty, I will never regain my consciousness.

_____
(Initial)

I suffer from advanced dementia or any other condition which results in the substantial loss of my cognitive ability and my health care providers determine that, to a high degree of medical certainty, this loss is not reversible.

2. These are My Directives about Prolonging My Life:

In those situations I have initialed in Section 1, I direct that my health care providers:

NOTE: INITIAL ONLY IN ONE PLACE.

_____
(Initial)

may withhold or withdraw life prolonging measures.

_____
(Initial)

shall withhold or withdraw life prolonging measures.

3. Exceptions – "Artificial Nutrition or Hydration"
NOTE: INITIAL ONLY IF YOU WANT TO MAKE EXCEPTIONS TO YOUR INSTRUCTIONS IN PARA-GRAPH 2.

EVEN THOUGH I do not want my life prolonged in those situations I have initialed in Section 1:

_____
(Initial)

I *DO* want to receive BOTH artificial hydration AND artificial nutrition (for example, through tubes) in those situations.

NOTE: DO NOT INITIAL THIS BLOCK IF ONE OF THE BLOCKS BELOW IS INITIALED.

_____
(Initial)

I *DO* want to receive ONLY artificial hydration (for example, through tubes) in those situations.

NOTE: DO NOT INITIAL THE BLOCK ABOVE OR BELOW IF THIS BLOCK IS INITIALED.

_____
(Initial)

I *DO* want to receive ONLY artificial nutrition (for example, through tubes) in those situations.

NOTE: DO NOT INITIAL EITHER OF THE TWO BLOCKS ABOVE IF THIS BLOCK IS INITIALED.

4. I Wish to be Made as Comfortable as Possible

I direct that my health care providers take reasonable steps to keep me as clean, comfortable, and free of pain as possible so my dignity is maintained, even though this care may hasten my death.

5. I Understand my Advance Directive

I am aware and understand that this document directs certain life prolonging measures to be withheld or discontinued in accordance with my advance instructions.

6. If I have an Available Health Care Agent

If I have appointed a health care agent by executing a health care power of attorney or similar instrument and that health care agent is acting and available and gives instructions that differ from this Advance Directive, then I direct that:

_____
(Initial)

Follow Advance Directive: This Advance Directive will override instructions my health care agent gives about prolonging my life.

_____
(Initial)

Follow Health Care Agent: My health care agent has authority to override this Advance Directive.

NOTE: DO NOT INITIAL BOTH BLOCKS. IF YOU DO NOT INITIAL EITHER BOX, YOUR HEALTH CARE PROVIDERS WILL FOLLOW THIS ADVANCE DIRECTIVE AND IGNORE THE INSTRUCTIONS OF YOUR HEALTH CARE AGENT ABOUT PROLONGING YOUR LIFE.

7. My Health Care Providers May Rely on this Directive

My health care providers shall not be liable to me or to my family, my estate, my heirs, or my personal representative for following the instructions I give in this instrument. Following my directions shall not be considered suicide, or the cause of my death, or malpractice, or unprofessional conduct. If I have revoked this instrument but my health care providers do not know that I have done so, and they follow the instructions in this instrument in good faith, they shall be entitled to the same protections to which they would have been entitled if the instrument had not been revoked.

8. I Want this Directive to be Effective Anywhere

I intend that this Advance Directive be followed by any health care provider in any place.

9. I have the Right to Revoke this Advance Directive

I understand that at any time I may revoke this Advance Directive in a writing I sign or by communicating in any clear and consistent manner my intent to revoke it to my attending physician. I understand that if I revoke this instrument, I should try to destroy all copies of it.

This the _____ day of _____, _____.

_____

PrintName_____

I hereby state that the declarant, _____, being of sound mind, signed (or directed another to sign on declarant's behalf) the foregoing Advance Directive for a Natural Death in my presence, and that I am not related to the declarant by blood or marriage, and I would not be entitled to any portion of the estate of the declarant under any existing will or codicil of the declarant or as an heir under the Intestate Succession Act, if the declarant died on this date without a will. I also state that I am not the declarant's attending physician, nor a licensed health care provider who is (1) an employee of the declarant's attending physician, (2) nor an employee of the health facility in which the declarant is a patient, or (3) an employee of a nursing home or any adult care home where the declarant resides. I further state that I do not have any claim against the declarant or the estate of the declarant.

Date:_____ Witness:_____

Date:_____ Witness:_____

_____COUNTY, _____STATE

Sworn to (or affirmed) and subscribed before me this day by

_____

(type/print name of declarant)

_____

(type/print name of witness)

_____

(type/print name of witness)

Date _____

                (Official Seal)

_____

Signature of Notary Public

_____, Notary Public

Printed or typed name

My commission expires: _____

Appendix D

Summary of Basic Will Information by State

State	Minimum Age to Make a Will	Nuncupative (Oral) Will Recognized	Holographic Will Recognized	Self-proving Affidavit Allowed	Self-proving Affidavit Form Provided by Statute
Alabama	18	No	No	Yes	Yes
Alaska	18	No	Yes	Yes	Yes
Arkansas	18	No	Yes	Yes	Yes
Arizona	18	No	Yes	Yes	Yes
California	18	No	Yes	Yes	Yes
Colorado	18	No	Yes	Yes	Yes
Connecticut	18	No	No	Yes	No
Delaware	18	No	No	Yes	Yes
District of Columbia	18	No	No	No	No
Florida	18	No	No	Yes	Yes
Georgia	14	No	No	Yes	Yes
Hawaii	18	No	Yes	Yes	Yes

State	Minimum Age to Make a Will	Nuncupative (Oral) Will Recognized	Holographic Will Recognized	Self-proving Affidavit Allowed	Self-proving Affidavit Form Provided by Statute
Idaho	18 (and emancipated minors)	No	Yes	Yes	Yes
Illinois	18	No	No	Yes	No
Indiana	18	No	Yes	Yes	Yes
Iowa	18	No	No	Yes	Yes
Kansas	18	Yes	No	Yes	Yes
Kentucky	18	No	No	Yes	Yes
Louisiana	16	No	Yes	No	No
Maine	18	No	Yes	Yes	Yes
Maryland	18	No	Yes (only if active military)	No	No
Massachusetts	18	No	No	Yes	Yes
Michigan	18	No	Yes	Yes	Yes
Minnesota	18	No	No	Yes	Yes
Mississippi	18	No	Yes	No	No
Missouri	18	No	No	Yes	Yes
Montana	18	No	Yes	Yes	No
Nebraska	18	No	Yes	Yes	Yes
Nevada	18	No	Yes	Yes	Yes
New Hampshire	18 (Younger if married)	No	No	Yes	Yes
New Jersey	18	No	Yes	Yes	Yes
New Mexico	18	No	No	Yes	Yes
New York	18	Yes	Yes	Yes	No
North Carolina	18	Yes	Yes	Yes	Yes

State	Minimum Age to Make a Will	Nuncupative (Oral) Will Recognized	Holographic Will Recognized	Self-proving Affidavit Allowed	Self-proving Affidavit Form Provided by Statute
North Dakota	18	No	Yes	Yes	Yes
Ohio	18	Yes	No	No	No
Oklahoma	18	Yes	Yes	Yes	Yes
Oregon	18	No	No	No	No
Pennsylvania	18	No	No	Yes	Yes
Rhode Island	18	No	No	Yes	Yes
South Carolina	18	No	No	Yes	Yes
South Dakota	18	No	Yes	Yes	Yes
Tennessee	18	Yes	Yes	No	No
Texas	18	No	No	Yes	Yes
Utah	18	No	Yes	Yes	Yes
Vermont	18	No	Yes	No	No
Virginia	18	No	Yes	Yes	Yes
Washington	18	Yes	No	No	No
West Virginia	18	No	No	No	No
Wisconsin	18	No	No	Yes	No
Wyoming	18	No	Yes	Yes	Yes

Glossary

401(k) plan: A retirement plan many people have from their employer, which usually involves contributions made by the employee; such plans can include an employer match of the employee contributions.

A

AB trust: Refers to either marital deduction or bypass trust.

Actuarial value: This is the value of the interest of a property or a right you as an individual own, and it is based on various life expectancy charts. A life estate is most often determined by the life expectancy of the particular person.

Ademption: When the bequest of a specific property in a will cannot be honored because the item has been either lost or sold before the person's death.

Adjustable life insurance policy: Allows the policy owner to change the plan of insurance, increase or decrease the face amount or premium, and lengthen or shorten the policy's period of protection.

Adjusted cost base: Used to determine what the capital gains or losses will be and the acquisition cost of a property plus the cost of any improvements to the property.

Administrator: The person who the court appoints to be in charge of an estate when there was no will or when the will does not name an executor. This person's title might also be a personal representative.

Advance medical directive (AMD): A document that covers a number of medical, legal, and ethical situations during a person's illness or death.

Affidavit: A written declaration made under oath or a written statement sworn to be true before someone legally authorized to administer an oath.

Alternative appointment: A secondary executor appointed in case the primary executor is unable or unwilling to perform his or her duties.

Alternative minimum tax (AMT): A federal tax that is part of the federal tax code. Taxpayers compute both the traditional income tax and the AMT and are responsible for paying whichever is higher. The AMT is calculated based on an expanded definition of taxable income, a larger exemption, and lower tax rates than those found in the traditional income tax.

Alternate valuation date: This date is no more than six months after the person in question's death; it is used to determine and evaluate the assets in an estate for federal estate tax purposes.

Agent: Refer to *attorney in fact*.

Ancillary probate: The probate for property that is owned in another state than where the person's primary residence was held.

Annuitant: The person who receives specific amounts of payment from an annuity; for example, a charitable gift annuity.

Annuity: Another investment type that involves a fixed amount of money for a specific number of years or for the life of the person taking out the annuity.

Appreciating asset: An asset with a value that has increased or continues to increase due to various reasons, for example, inflation. The term used might also simply be referred to as appreciated.

Assets: A person's property or items with value.

Attorney: A person authorized to practice law and give legal advice.

Attorney in fact: The person who is authorized by a power of attorney to act on another person's behalf. This person might also be called the agent, or in the case of health care directives, surrogate or proxy.

Augmented estate: The sum total of what a person owns; includes both probate and nonprobate items in the estate. This might be used when determining a surviving spouse's elective share.

Autopsy: When a person's body is examined after he or she is dead, usually determining the cause of death to verify the diagnosis given.

B

Basic will: A simple will that distributes everything to the living spouse or the children if the spouse is dead or to another single individual.

Beneficiary: The person who is named in the will or trust to receive money or assets belonging to the deceased.

Bequest: The gift someone is left of personal property outlined in the will.

Buy-sell agreement: A contract made between two people who are either partners or owners of a business in which certain conditions are decided upon and a price for a buyout is agreed upon by the partners at the time of death or retirement of the other partner.

Bypass trust: Also referred to as a credit shelter trust or the B subtrust of an AB living trust. It contains the federal estate tax protected amount and is not taxed.

C

Cafeteria plan: Also known as a "fringe benefit" for an employee and allows the employer to decide on the various tax-free and taxed benefits for the employee.

Capital: Money or property owned by a person who has economic value.

Capital beneficiary: A beneficiary entitled to the capital of a trust.

Capital cost allowance: A Canadian formula for claiming depreciation expenses.

Capital gain: The difference between what an asset is sold for and its original purchase price.

Capital gains tax: A federal levy on profits from the sale of a person's property and is the difference between the sale price and what the owner's tax basis on the property is after the sale.

Capital loss: The loss incurred when a capital asset is sold for a lower price than the purchase price.

Cash surrender value: The amount of money a person will receive from an insurance company if a life insurance policy is canceled prior to the death of the insured party.

Cash surrender value insurance: What is known as life insurance with a savings account including coverage for the lifetime of the insured person.

Charitable gift annuity (CGA): An arrangement where a qualified charitable organization receives an initial investment from the donor and agrees to make a regular, fixed-sum annuity to the donor over his or her lifetime. When the donor dies, the charity keeps the original investment.

Charitable lead trust: A gift made in trust to a charity; this includes the income payable to the charity for a specified amount of time. The remainder of the money is then returned to the donor or to another noncharity.

Charitable remainder trust: A gift made in trust to a charity that includes income payable to the donor during the donor's lifetime. When the donor dies, the remainder of the monies goes to the charity.

Claim: In asset protection planning, it is the right to payment, even if disputed.

Codicil: A written change to an existing will that is legally witnessed.

Common law: A law in many states in which marital property ownership is split up.

Community property: A law that says any property or assets acquired after a marriage are owned equally and jointly by both spouses; this law is recognized in nine states.

Community property agreement: A document that legally transfers the title of a property owned by both spouses over to the surviving spouse.

Condominium: A situation in which several people

own property in the same building, and there is an equal interest involved for everyone owning the property.

Consanguinity: Genetic relationship in which an individual that is a blood relative of another has at least one common ancestor in the preceding few generations.

Conservatorship: The custody or control of a person's money and property as named by the court.

Continuing power of attorney: An enduring, or durable, power of attorney that remains effective even if the person conferring the power becomes mentally incapable.

Cooperative: A style of buying housing in which several different people buy shares in an entity that owns the building. Shareholders who are also tenants in the building hold a proprietary lease that gives them the rights to the units in which they live.

Coverdell education savings account (ESA): A savings account created to pay for legitimate educational expenses with a maximum yearly contribution being $2,000, which can change from year to year.

Creator: The person who creates the trust who might also be called the settlor, grantor, or trustor.

Credit life insurance: A certain type of insurance that is bought by mortgagors, as it will pay off a mortgage debt if the person dies.

Creditor: A person or company who has made a claim for payment.

Current assumption whole life insurance: A variation of an ordinary life insurance policy where the cash values are based on the individual's current mortality, investment, and expenses. This account is credited with a current interest rate that changes over time.

Custodian: The person who is the trustee of any Uniform Transfers to Minors Act (UTMA) account whether it is money or property.

D

Deferred gift: A donation to charity that you make plans for now but pay in the future. It is usually paid after death.

Dependent life insurance: Group life insurance that covers the spouse, children, or other dependents of the group member.

Devise: A gift given by a person's will.

Devolve: Pass on or delegate a power, asset, or responsibility to another.

Disability: A physical or mental impairment that limits major life activities, such as caring for one's self, walking, seeing, hearing, speaking, breathing, learning, working, or receiving education.

Domicile: A person's residence that he or she considers his or her primary or permanent address and home.

Donee: The person who receives any sort of gift.

Donor: The person who gives any sort of gift.

Durable power of attorney: A document by which a person gives a second person full legal authority to act on the first person's behalf even if the first person becomes mentally incompetent.

E

Elective share: A state-specific share of a deceased person's estate and thus given to the surviving spouse instead of whatever the inheritance in the will might have been; also referred to as forced share.

Endowment fund: A fund where the principal investment is used for ongoing business operations or related expenses; this type of fund is generally used by universities, hospitals, and nonprofits.

Enduring power of attorney: A legal document granting a person the authority to act on your behalf in legal or business matters if you are incapable of doing so.

Escheat: An instance in which property is given to the government when the owner dies because there are no heirs and no will is left behind.

Estate: All the property and valuable things a person owns.

Estate freeze: A technique used to transfer assets to an individual's beneficiaries while reducing estate taxes.

Estate planning: The process of arranging for the distribution of one's assets.

Estate tax: A federal and state tax that taxes the transfer of wealth upon death.

Ethical will: A non-legal document, which might also be a video from a person to his or her loved ones, telling those living his or her wishes and things he or she learned in life.

Exclusions and limitations: Medical services that are not covered or limited in benefit by a person's insurance policy.

Executor: A person or institution that has been named to be in charge of the will to carry out the provisions made by the deceased. Also called executrix when a female is named.

Executor misconduct: Any action that violates the executor's legal duty to act in the best interest of testator under the terms of the will and in accordance with law.

F

Fair market value: For estate purposes, the IRS defines fair market value as follows: "The fair market value is the price at which the property would change hands between a willing buyer and a willing seller, neither being under any compulsion to buy or to sell and both having reasonable knowledge of relevant facts.
The fair market value of a particular item of property includable in the decedent's gross estate is not to be determined by a forced sale price. Nor is the fair market value of an item of property to be determined by the sale price of the item in a market other than that in which such item is most commonly sold to the public, taking into account the location of the item wherever appropriate." IRS Reg. §20.2031-1.

Family income life insurance:
A form of insurance where a lump sum is paid when the insured dies plus income to help support the family of the deceased.

Family limited partnership (FLP): This is a limited partnership in which the partners are a closely related group or family.

Fiduciary: A person who is designated to act on behalf of another, which requires both confidence and in good faith, such as a trustee or executor.

Forced share: Refer to *elective share*.

Fraudulent transfer: The transfer made by a person with the intent to hinder or delay a creditor.

Future interest: A property interest that allows for the future possession or use. For example, a remainder interest in a trust would fall into this category.

G

General power of attorney: A formal agreement that

allows you to appoint someone to take care of your financial and business affairs when you are no longer able to do so.

Generation skipping tax: An extra levy that is in addition to the gift or estate tax on gifts to grandchildren or other generational heirs.

Gift: Completed lifetime transfer of money or property to another person or a charitable organization.

Gift in kind: A gift that is anything other than money.

Gift tax: The federal tax rendered on money or property gifted by one person to another that is not specifically excluded from being taxed by law.

Grantor: Also called a settler or trustor; the person who creates a trust. A grantor can also be one who conveys property to another.

Gross estate: The total value of a person's estate without

accounting for debts and taxes that may be owed.

Group life insurance: What is known as term life insurance given at a group rate, usually through an employer benefit plan.

Guardian: The person who is legally responsible for handling the affairs and/ or care of a minor child or person deemed incompetent. A guardian is appointed by the court.

H

Health care agent: A person who is given authority in the situation of an advanced medical directive to make the health care decisions when one becomes unable to do so for himself or herself. This person might also be referred to as health care surrogate or health care proxy.

Health care power of attorney: A document that provides authority to another person to make medical decisions on behalf of the person executing the document. See also Durable power of attorney.

Heir: The person or persons entitled to inherit by law.

Holographic will: A will that is written entirely in the handwriting of the person making the will, with no witnesses. This type of will is not valid in all states.

I

Incapable/incompetent: Unable to act on one's own behalf due to the inability to do so on a day-to-day basis as determined by medical providers and, in some states, by court decision.

Incentive trust provision: A clause in a will or trust that provides a certain reward to a beneficiary for fulfilling the wishes of the testator or trust grantor; for example, graduating from school or getting married.

Incidence of ownership: An insurance term that normally refers to the person considered the owner, that is, who has the power over the policy's continuation and designation of beneficiaries.

Individual retirement account (IRA): A retirement account created by a person, not an employer; contributions the owner makes to the account will also be tax deductible as determined by law.

Inheritance tax: A tax that certain states levy on the beneficiaries for property they inherit. The amount of tax generally is scaled according to the relationship of the person receiving the property to the deceased.

Imputed interest: The rate of interest assigned by the Internal Revenue Service to a loan that is given at less than the market rate or as a no-interest loan. The lender must pay taxes on the interest even if no money was received from the borrower, who is usually a family member.

Inter vivos trust: A trust created while an individual is still alive to hold property for the benefit of another.

Intestate: When a person dies without a will.

Irrevocable life insurance trust (ILIT): Any irrevocable trust that owns life insurance.

Irrevocable trust: A trust with fixed terms that cannot be revoked or changed by the grantor in any significant way.

J

Joint tenancy with right of survivorship: When a property is owned jointly between two or more people with the right of survivorship taking precedence as necessary. The survivorship interest passes outside of probate.

K

Kiddie tax: A term loosely used for federal income tax on minors under the age of 14 years old.

L

Legacy: The property or money bequeathed to someone in a will.

Life estate: The income from a trust account; it is good as long as the person who holds the interest is alive. Might also refer to real estate language in which ownership is divided equally in two and one half is the length of the homeowner's life while the other half is the part willed to the heir, therefore becoming the heirs at the time that the owner of the property dies.

Life insurance: A contract one makes with an insurance company for a specified amount of money to be paid to beneficiaries named when the insured person dies.

Life interest: Property interest payable during the owner's lifetime or other property rights that a person holds only during his or her lifetime.

Life support: Medical equipment that assists or replaces bodily functions necessary to keep a person alive.

Life-prolonging (or life-sustaining) efforts:
A medical procedure or treatment using artificial means to keep a person alive when his or her organs stop working and that only serves to prolong the dying process. This does not include medication or procedures that alleviate pain.

Life tenant: A person who is legally entitled to the use of real estate or the income from real estate as long as he or she is alive.

Limited liability company (LLC): A form of business entity created by state law to combine the liability

protection and other features of a traditional corporation with the tax features of a partnership.

Limited partnership: A business entity in which the owners or limited partners share profits and losses but do not take part in the day-to-day management of the business and so are only exposed to limited liability under state law for problems against the business should it arise.

Limited power of attorney: A legal document that only grants the attorney in fact power to do specified things for the person who names him or her.

Living trust: Can either be irrevocable or revocable and is a written agreement that a person known as the settlor or grantee has in which he or she can transfer assets and property with specific instructions to the trustee for the management of the future distribution of all assets.

Living will: An advance medical directive in which a person puts in writing his or her wishes regarding medical treatment at the end of his or her life in case he or she cannot communicate those wishes otherwise.

M

Marital deduction: A federal estate tax deduction that involves the property the deceased spouse receives; also referred to as a bypass trust or an AB trust.

Marital deduction trust: A trust both written and funded so it is eligible for the state tax unlimited marital deduction upon the death of the grantor or spouse.

Medicaid: A state-run medical program that receives federal and state contributions and takes care of the payments of both senior citizens and others without the means to pay for their medical care.

Medicare: A federally run program that helps the elderly pay for their medical expenses.

Mental incapacity: The inability of a person to make reasoned decisions or understand his or her circumstances because of a mental disorder.

N

Natural death: Death by causes other than accident or homicide.

Next of kin: The nearest blood relative of the person who has died.

No-contest clause: A clause inserted into a will to exclude anyone who challenges the will in court from receiving a gift under the will. This clause is also known as an *in terrorem* clause. The clause is meant to discourage beneficiaries from challenging the will in court.

No will: When a person dies without a will and his or her estate passes to heirs based on the laws of descent and distribution of the state of his or her residence. *See also intestate.*

Nonprobate property: Property that passes in ownership by a vehicle outside the probate process, such as life insurance, proceeds directly to a beneficiary, a joint survivorship interest, or living trust.

Notarized or notarial copy: A document that has been certified valid by a notary public who has witnessed the signing of the document or has reviewed the original.

P

Pay-on-death (POD): An account or other property in which a person is named to receive it upon the death of the owner.

Payback supplemental-needs trust (SNT): When public funds are used for a disabled person's care and then paid back from a trust after the disabled beneficiary dies.

Per stirpes: A method of distributing an estate whereby each generational level of a family receives an equal share of the decedent's estate.

Persistent vegetative state: A condition where a patient cannot speak, follow simple commands, or respond in any conscious way. This can also be when a person is in a coma with no awareness of his or her surroundings. This condition is certified by physicians.

Personal care: Assisting someone who needs help walking, bathing, or cooking; usually done by individuals trained specifically for this job who might or might not have medical backgrounds.

Personal property: Property that is movable and can be as diverse as furniture, cars, jewelry, and also property that represents an interest in other intangible property, such as bank accounts or mutual funds.

Personal representative: A person appointed to manage another's affairs and estate; can also be called the executor or administrator.

Pickup tax: An estate tax that is levied by certain states, but not all, to the federal state death tax credit.

Pooled income trust: Charitable remainder trust where cash and securities are available and combined with various contributions from other people and then managed like a mutual fund.

Posthumous conception: Conception of a child that occurs after the death of the parent. This type of conception occurs when the sperm or ova of one of the parents have been frozen and are used to conceive a child through in vitro fertilization after the parent's death; frozen embryos preserved by a couple can also be used for such conception.

Pour-over will: A type of will created to cover property that is not transferred to a living trust. Instead a trust is created by assets designated in the will.

Power of attorney (POA): A legal document authorizing someone to act on behalf of another.

Precedent: An example used to justify similar occurrences at a later time.

Prenuptial agreement: An agreement two people sign before getting married describing what each person's rights are regarding property and what each person will receive at the time of death of the spouse or in the case of a divorce.

Probatable assets: Assets that are part of a deceased person's estate and are named in the will. This includes all property owned by the decedent that has not been transferred in some other way prior to death, such as by joint survivorship interests, gifts, and trusts.

Probate court: A specialized court set up to handle the management of wills and estates of persons who die within their jurisdiction, with or without a will. These courts also handle guardianships.

Probate estate: The assets of the deceased distributed under the direction of the probate court.

Prudent investor rule: A state law outlining the obligations and standards that must be followed by an executor or trustee when managing investments under his or her control.

Q

Qualified terminal interest property (QTIP) trust: A marital trust that allows the estate to receive the marital deduction even though the spouse who has survived only has an income interest in the trust.

Qualified retirement plan: A plan that allows for a special tax treatment with contributions made to the plan and the income earned during the existence of the plan. Examples are 401(k) plans or defined plans.

R

Real property: Includes land and buildings as well as anything attached to or growing from the land, such as a lake or trees.

Remainder interest: Property most likely left in a trust to another person after the death of the person who has an income interest in that property.

Remainderman: In a life estate, one or more people designated by the original property owner to receive the property once the life estate owner dies.

Renewable term insurance:
Term insurance that can be
renewed at the end of the
term if the policy owner
wants to renew it without
evidence of insurability for a
limited number of successive
terms.

**Required minimum
distribution (RMD):**
The smallest amount of a
yearly distribution allowed
by law in regards to a
retirement account.

Residue: An old legal term
that refers to anything
remaining in a person's
probate estate after the
payment of legal obligations
and the distributions have
been made as requested in
the will.

Revocable trust: A trust that
the grantor can terminate or
change at any time.

Right of election: The right
of the surviving spouse
to denounce the deceased
person's will and take a
state-specified share of the
deceased's estate.

Right of occupancy: A grant
of property rights that ends
when the right-holder is
no longer occupying the
property.

Roth IRA: An individual
retirement account that has
nondeductible contributions
and earnings, which are
tax free.

S

Second-to-die life insurance:
Insurance that insures two
people and pays benefits only
after the second person dies.

Self-proving will: A
statement appended to a
will attested before a notary
public or other person
authorized to administer
oaths that affirm the testator's
and witnesses' signatures
to the will. This document
authenticates the will so the
witnesses will not be required
to appear in probate court to
verify the document after the
testator dies.

Separate property: A property owned by one of the spouses that is not part of the joint estate or belonging to the couple as community property.

Settlement: The completion of all items being distributed appropriately.

Settlor: One term for the person who funds a trust. This person is also called a grantor or trustor.

Specific bequest: The gift of a named item in a will to a certain person.

Specific devise: A gift named in a will for an item of any kind. See also Specific bequest.

Spendthrift trust: This trust creates a beneficiary who does not have money management abilities, therefore preventing the beneficiary from spending inheritance money unwisely.

Spousal trust: A trust that entitles the spouse to all income for his or her lifetime.

Springing power of attorney: Alternative to the durable power of attorney that only becomes effective, *i.e.,* "springs" into action, upon the principal's disability and does not take effect upon signing.

State death taxes: Taxes that a state imposes on a deceased person's property after his or her death depending on the state in which he or she lived.

Survivorship insurance: Insurance that pays a death benefit upon the death of the last surviving insured person. Married couples use this method in estate planning, and it might also be called dual-life insurance or second-to-die insurance.

Supervised procedure: A formal probate court procedure in which any action carried out on behalf of the estate is supervised by the court. This is opposite of what is called an unsupervised or limited supervision probate.

Successor trustee: The person who takes over as the trustee if the original trustee does not or cannot serve in this role, such as because of death or incompetency.

Supplemental needs trust (SNT): A trust whose sole beneficiary is a disabled person receiving government assistance; also referred to as a special-needs trust.

T

Tax basis: Value of property for tax purposes. For example, property that is improved such as adding a building to open land increases in value. Valuation for tax purposes can be adjusted for with offset for depreciation.

Taxable estate: The total value of a deceased individual's assets, which are subject to taxation minus their liabilities and any tax-deductible portions of these assets.

Tenancy in common: The co-ownership of a property title without the right of survival, which means a co-owner can leave his or her part of the property to any person he or she chooses.

Tenancy in the entirety: The joint ownership of property limited to married couples; this includes the right of survivorship. This is not available in all states and has been phased out in some states that used to allow for it.

Term life insurance: Insurance coverage without any savings program added.

Terminally ill: When a person has an incurable illness and will only live a short time as determined with reasonable medical certainty.

Testamentary trust: A trust created in the deceased person's will.

Testamentary capacity: A state law requirement that the person making the will be of sound mind when creating and signing the will.

Testator: A person who writes his or her will.

Transfer: Change in ownership of an asset or interest in an asset.

Transfer-on-death (TOD): A brokerage or mutual fund or other account or asset that a person names beneficiaries for and who will receive the asset upon his or her death; ownership passes outside of probate.

Trust: A written and legal document that designates a person or group of people to hold property and manage it as necessary on behalf of the identified beneficiaries in accordance with the trust as specified by the specific instructions of the person who created the trust.

Trust agreement: A document that gives the instructions for how to manage a property left in the living trust; also instructs who will receive portions of the trust assets.

Trustee: A person or institution granted authority to manage the trust property as set forth in the trust agreement.

Trustor: The person who creates the trust; also known as the grantor, settlor, or creator.

Trust principal: Any type of property — including a financial account or real estate — transferred to the trustee to manage on behalf of the trust.

Trust protector: The person given the authority by the trust grantor to make decisions regarding the beneficiaries and to monitor the trustee's performance.

U

Undue influence: When a person is in a close

relationship with the person making the will and uses mental coercion over this person while he or she is writing his or her will, which therefore means the will does not really reflect the testator's true wishes.

Unitrust: A type of charitable trust in which the donor receives at least a minimum yearly return based on the annual value of the assets.

V

Valuation planning: Legal and financial strategies that help to decrease the value of the property transferred by a lifetime gift or upon death for federal gift or estate tax purposes.

Viatical settlement: An insurance payout for those who have terminal illnesses, which allows the person to draw advance monies on the insurance proceeds that would normally be paid after the person is dead.

Vicarious liability: A personal liability that arises from malpractice or negligence of one's employees or others in an organization.

W

Waiver of premium: A clause in an insurance policy that stops collection of the insurance premiums if the insured becomes seriously ill or disabled.

Will: A legal document directing how a person's property and assets should be distributed and other estate matters handled upon the person's upon death.

Will contest: When a will's validity or certain provisions of a will are challenged in court by someone claiming an interest in the testator's estate.

Bibliography

Anmal Legal & Historical Center. **www.animallaw.info./articles/armpuspettrusts.htm**. Accessed on December 19, 2010.

Brown, Richard Lewis. "The Holograph Problem – The Case Against Holographic Wills," 75 *Tenn. L. Rev.* 93 (2006-2007).

Campbell, Brett. *The American Bar Association Guide to Wills & Estates* 2d ed. New York: Random House, 2004.

Copeland & Tierman, LLP. "Estate Tax Changes Under the 2010 Tax Relief Act." December 2010. **www.copelandtierman.net/News/Estate%20Tax%20Update%20%20December%202010.aspx**. Accessed on January 9. 2011.

Davis. Matt. "Life insurance: How much is enough?" 2011. **www.money-tips.com.au/articles/8/1/Life-Insurance-How-much-is-enough-/Page1.html**. Accessed on January 17, 2011.

"How to Get Married in Massachusetts." GLAD. June, 2010.
www.glad.org/uploads/docs/publications/how-to-get-married-ma.pdf. Accessed on January 6, 2011.

"Estate tax." Internal Revenue Service. October 21, 2008.
www.irs.gov/businesses/small/article/0,,id=164871,00.html.
Accessed on December 13, 2010.

"Frequently Asked Questions on Estate Taxes." Internal
Revenue Service. **www.irs.gov/businesses/small/
article/0,,id=108143,00.html#2**. Accessed on January 9, 2011.

"Form 706. United States Estate (and Generation-Skipping
Transfer) Tax Return." Revision as of 9/2009, for use through
12/31/2010. Internal Revenue Service. **www.irs.gov/pub/irs-pdf/f706.pdf**. Accessed on January 9, 2011.

"Funeral Service Facts." National Funeral Directors Association,
2011. **www.nfda.org/media-center/statisticsreports.html**.
Accessed on January 17, 2011.

Garber, Julie. "Overview of Current Federal Estate Tax
Laws. Where Will Congress Go From Here?" About.
com Wills & Estate Planning. **http://wills.about.com/od/
understandingestatetaxes/a/overviewfed.htm**.
Accessed on January 8, 2011.

Garber, Julie. "What is the Future of the Federal Estate Tax?"
About.com Wills & Estate Planning. **http://wills.about.com/od/
understandingestatetaxes/a/futureoftax.htm**.
Accessed on January 9, 2011.

Geller, Bradley. "Advance Directives: Planning for Medical Care in the Event of Loss of Decision-making Ability." State Bar of Michigan.
http://michbar.org/elderlaw/adpamphlet.cfm.
Accessed on December 19, 2010.

"Gift Tax." Internal Revenue Service. October 21, 2008.
www.irs.gov/businesses/small/article/0,,id=164872,00.html.
Accessed on December 13, 2010.

Harris, Virgil M. *Ancient Curious and Famous Wills*. Boston: Little, Brown, 1911.

Hill v. Davis & Cobb v. Same (2 cases), 64 Okla. 253, 1917 LEXIS 637 (1917). Accessed LEXIS on December 23, 2010.
(Re: competency of witnesses for valid will.)

In re Estate of Timmons, 2000 Mich. App. LEXIS 1642 (2000). Accessed LEXIS on December 23, 2010. (Re: undue influence and coercion on testator.)

Kraft, Paul A. "What is a Reciprocal Will?" June 11, 2010.
http://blog.frankkraft.com/2010/06/reciprocal.
Accessed on December 19, 2010.

"Last Will and Testament of Elvis A. Presley." **www.ibiblio.org/elvis/elvwill.html**. Accessed on January 15, 2011.

"Last Will and Testament of George Washington." **www.pbs.org/georgewashington/collection/other_last_will.html**.
Accessed on December 19, 2010.

"Last Will and Testament of John F. Kennedy." **www.rongolini. com/jfk.htm**. Accessed on January 17, 2011.

"Last Will and Testament of John Winston Ono Lennon." The Lectric Law Library. **www.lectlaw.com/files/cur42.htm**. Accessed on January 17, 2011.

"Last Will and Testament of Paul Newman." Living Trust Network. **www.livingtrustnetwork.com/estate-planning-center/last-will-and-testament/wills-of-the-rich-and-famous/last-will-and-testament-of-paul-newman.html**. Accessed on January 18, 2011.

"Last Will and Testament of Walter E. Disney." Living Trust Network. **http://livingtrustnetwork.com/index. php?option=com_content&task=view&id=103&Itemid=44**. Accessed on January 17, 2011.

Maple, Stephen. *The Complete Idiot's Guide to Wills & Estates*, 3d ed. New York: Penguin, 2005.

Martinez, Jose. "Leona Helmsley's will to give $1 million to dog causes, down from $12m." *The NY Daily News*. April 21, 2009. **www.nydailynews.com/gossip/2009/04/22/2009-04-22_man_bites_dog_over_leona_will_judge_cuts_pooch_share_from_12m_to_1m.html**. Accessed on December 19, 2010.

Palermo, Michael T. *AARP Crash Course in Estate Planning*. New York: Sterling, 2005.

Pence v. Waugh, 135 Ind. 143, 1893 Ind. LEXIS 201 (1893). Accessed LEXIS on December 23, 2010. (Re: purpose of attesting witnesses to will; and law presumes sanity of testator.)

Polasky, Alan N. "Pour-Over Wills: Use with Intervivos Trusts." 17 *Sw. L.J. 410* (1963).

"Requirements for a Will." LivingTrustNetwork.com. **http.//livingtrustnetwork.com/estate-planning-center/ last-will-and-testament/requirements-for-a-will.html**. Accessed on December 31, 2010.

"Tax Relief Act of 2010, Enacted December 17, 2010." **www.taxtrustsandestateslawmonitor.com/2010/12/articles/ estate-tax/tax-relief-act-of-2010-enacted-december-17-2010**. Accessed on January 15, 2010.

"The Whys and Hows of Wills." AARP.org, November 2008. **www.aarp.org/money/estate-planning/info-11-2008/whys_ hows_wills.html**. Accessed on December 13, 2010.

"Wills laws – Information on the law about wills." **http://law.jrank.org/pages/11862/Wills.html**. Accessed on December 18, 2010.

Wolf, Susan M. *et al.* "Sources of Concern about the Patient Self-Determination Act." *The New England Journal of Medicine.* December 15, 1991: 1666-1671. **www.nejm.org/doi/full/10.1056/ NEJM199112053252334**. Accessed on January 11, 2011.

Author Biographies

L inda C. Ashar is a practicing attorney with 25 years experience. She is also an educator, freelance writer, artist, and breeder of Morgan horses and Irish pony breeds, including the critically endangered Kerry Bog Pony. She is a senior counsel in the law firm of Wickens, Herzer, Panza, Cook & Batista of Avon, Ohio, a visiting professor at DeVry University, and owner of Thornapple Farms in Vermilion, Ohio, with her husband Michael. She teaches legal seminars, has published many articles and poetry in journals and magazines, and has displayed her art in gallery exhibits. She also authored *101 Ways to Score Higher on Your LSAT* (Atlantic Publishing, 2008). When not involved in one of these many pursuits, you are likely to find Ashar visiting her favorite haunts with camera in hand on the shore of the Irish Sea in North Ireland or in Connemara and County Kerry in the west of Ireland. You can find out more on her website (**www.lindacashar.com**) or through e-mail at ashar@hbr.net.

andy Baker is a published author of several financial books, including, *Your Complete Guide to Early Retirement: A Step-By-Step Plan for Making It Happen* and *The Complete Guide to Planning Your Estate: A Step By Step Plan to Protect Your Assets, Limit Your Taxes, and Ensure Your Wishes Are Fulfilled.*

Sandy Baker is a mother of three and wife to an ever-supportive husband. She has provided full-time freelance writing for the last six years and writes about topics she finds fascinating.

Index